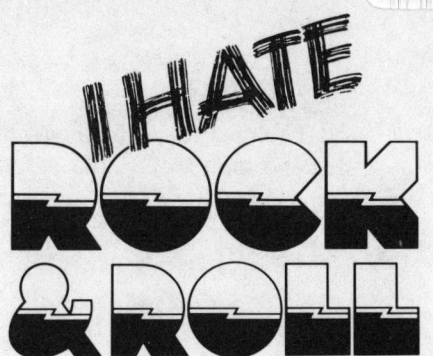

Tony Tyler

VERMILION
London Melbourne Sydney Auckland Johannesburg

Vermilion & Company Ltd

An imprint of the Hutchinson Publishing Group
17–21 Conway Street, London W1P 6JD

Hutchinson Group (Australia) Pty Ltd
30–32 Cremorne Street, Richmond South, Victoria 3121
PO Box 151, Broadway, New South Wales 2007

Hutchinson Group (NZ) Ltd
32–34 View Road, PO Box 40–086, Glenfield, Auckland 10

Hutchinson Group (SA) Pty Ltd
PO Box 337, Bergvlei 2012, South Africa

First published 1984

Set in Linotron Times by
Input Typesetting Ltd, London

Printed and bound in Great Britain by
Anchor Brendon Ltd,
Tiptree, Essex

ISBN 0 09 155791 7

CONTENTS

For Fang, and also for
'Dancing Dave' Hill
Not only cathartic, but seminal

ILLUSTRATIONS

ACKNOWLEDGEMENTS

Much as I'd like to take all the credit for this volume (I certainly intend to take all the money), common decency – oh all right, a well-developed tactical sense – obliges me to make obeisances in various directions.

My thanks to Neil Spencer and Fiona Foulgar at *New Musical Express* for allowing me to quote from the truly astonishing Paul Morley piece (pp. 68–9) and for allowing me access to their picture archives.

Secondly, may rich blessings be showered upon my agent Michael Thomas (of A. M. Heath & Co., reasonable rates) for valiantly getting this book past the project stage and into contractual status; and in the same connection, upon my editor at Vermilion, Susan Hill, for possessing exactly the right kind of outlook on life – which enabled her to see, at a glance, the dazzling merits of the Great Work.

I am also grateful to Faber and Faber for permission to quote from *Twilight of The Gods: The Beatles in Retrospect* by Wilfrid Mellers and to Jonathan Cape Ltd for allowing me to quote from *Girl, 20* by Kingsley Amis.

Finally, a deep and sincere tribute to the Olivetti Company, makers of the world's best electronic typewriter. May this book help me to pay for it.

1 September 1983

FOREWORD

Most books have titles that are self-explanatory. So does this one.*
That being so, why have I bothered to supply a Foreword?

The answer is simple. Existing books about current or past aspects
of rock subculture are so uncritical, so supinely self-limiting in their
collective refusal to confront obvious assumptions, so fantastically
simple-minded in the way they obligingly provide detailed exegeses for
every conceivable facet of the most supremely irrelevant phenomenon
of modern times that (for me at least) the inescapable conclusion is
this: the purchasers, as well as the authors and compilers – though not
the editors or publishers – of rock books comprise an identifiable group
of dullards fully capable of grossly misinterpreting even the simplest of
everyday phrases. In a hostile and uncomprehending world, nothing
can be left to chance. I cannot allow the possibility to arise that my
motives for writing this little book should be misunderstood, despite
the (to me, at least) unequivocal title.

Let me therefore declare immediately that *I Hate Rock and Roll*
owes its origins – or 'concept', if you prefer the jargon – to my long
immersion in almost wholly negative emotions; malice, spite and resentment mostly. These are the inevitable product of long brooding
on my own ridiculous failures in the boggy fields of the biz. Let there
be no mistake. *I Hate Rock and Roll* is not intended to pose as an
objective or even permissibly subjective assessment of the industry. It
is intended to be seen for what it is: a bitter, vituperative, biased,
obsessive, nasty, bad-tempered, unpleasant and selective snarl of pure
hatred at the rock business and all it has come to encompass in the
first lamentable twenty-five years or so of its existence.

I freely confess – I flaunt the fact – that I myself wasted more than
a decade of a miserably short lifespan foolishly engaged on what I'm

*Other examples: *The Forsyte Saga; A History of Torture.*

obliged to term 'rock pursuits'. I have been a lead guitarist but was hindered in my career by a profound inability to progress beyond a certain level of accomplishment, as well as a bourgeois reluctance to 'let it all hang out' on the public stage. Convinced, nevertheless, of my innate musicality, I abandoned the guitar in favour of the mighty Hammond organ. I didn't play this too well either, but it enabled me to sit down while performing and thus to avoid having to twitch, as is *de rigueur* for all perpendicular performances in this genre. Alas, the Hammond fell from favour – which for me was at least convenient, considering my own much-loved instrument had recently been stolen from me (in Italy, and, what is still more shaming, by an Italian).

Deposed thus by circumstance, not to mention the immutable laws of survival, from the front line of rock and roll, I spent a year sunk in self-indulgent navel contemplation; my Late Hippie period. I then decided to make use of another fancied talent, and turned to (*soi-disant*) rock journalism. My beginnings in this tawdry trade were humble enough; as the chief scapegoat (i.e. 'editor') of a two-bit, tradition-less, advertising-obsessed trade journal, a seedy monthly with a staff of two. Finally driven – from shame – to abandon this snakepit, I took an ill-advised running leap and landed even deeper in the silage. I became a PR man and all-purpose toady for one of Britain's more offensive, crass, morally reprehensible and all-round-disgusting tech-noflash combos. Humiliated beyond endurance, as were all employees of this loathsome cabal, the worm – and, by God, the cap fits – finally turned. One wild January day I walked out. Within a few days a failing music weekly, down to its last twelve issues unless its fortunes reversed themselves in their tracks – and at the time frantically hiring any 'journalist' whose knuckles didn't exactly touch the floor – had hired me; and I went on a handsome stipend to the world's largest, most successful and unprincipled magazine-publishing combine. I had arrived.

Curiously enough it was around this time that the scales, as the aphorism has it, began to fall from my eyes.

We were at the printers. The then editor and I were standing around, blearily examining the front cover, which at that stage needed only editorial approval before being passed for print and vanishing deep into the bowels of the print room. It had been a long, weary and indescribably trivial day, and we were in a condition of blind fatigue. We stood there mute, peering at the cover, checking it for the more absurd sorts of error (like the wrong century in the dateline) and simultaneously flogging our brains into cold, commercial assessment of the cover's supposed pulling power, consumerwise.

The cover photograph – that is to say, 80 per cent of the cover itself – consisted of a large, grotesque picture of one Dave Hill, the lead guitarist of a then-popular British group called (somewhat enigmatically, I always felt) Slade. Let me say at once that The Slade (as I prefer to call them) were never in my big league of unpleasant clowns. They dressed in a silly and uncomfortable manner (but who doesn't these days?), were quite unblessed by good looks (especially true, alas, of Dave Hill), but in their lead singer they boasted a vocalist of unusual power and clarity. Anyway, there we were, the then editor and I, staring glassily at the grisly likeness of Dave Hill. Hill is afflicted with conspicuously rodent-like molars, poor chap, and moreover in those days (early 1972) wore his hair in a very unfetching basin cut with ratty strands pendant behind. Worse, his stage clothing was ridiculous to the point of *prima facie* insanity; a pair of silver lamé overalls, striped football socks, glitter-dusted eyelids and fantastic platform-soled 'shoes'. Frozen in time,* Dave Hill of The Slade pranced all over our front cover like a volcanic combination of coypu and Christmas Tree: an image of wonder and despair.

Looking back, the odd thing was that neither the then editor nor I immediately recognized the innate fatuousness of the enterprise in which we were engaged. Solemnly we stood and passed comments like 'Striking' – 'Could move a bit to the left, don't you think?' – 'No, I don't think' – 'Well, you're probably right' . . . for all the world as if we were actually doing something worthwhile. As I have explained, it had been a tiring day.

Then it came. I was struck, pierced through by a sudden shaft of clear, empathetic insight, the product, no doubt, of the acute perceptivity that fatigue can sometimes bestow. It took the form of a deep, profound sorrow, a welling surge of pity for the berk Hill, induced thus to cavort like a badly operated marionette – and, what was more, have his shame broadcast to the vast readership of our journal. I felt my heart lurch.

Intending to strike a corresponding note of sympathy in the steely, cynical soul of the then editor, I murmured, in low tones: 'What a way to make a living!'

He did not immediately respond – in words, that is. After some moments I became uneasily aware that he had begun to shake. Convulsions? I eyed the man sharply. Then it dawned on me that he was laughing, positively racked with mirth at the predicament of the hapless Hill. After a short, self-righteous interval, I suddenly took his point. I now began to laugh. Once launched down this greasy slope we were quite unable to regain equilibrium. I'm afraid we caused a scene on the composing-room floor. Ruthless compositors slackened their

*It should be noted that in November 1983 The Slade released a 'comeback' single – their first for some years. It wasn't half bad.

prognathous mandibles in amazement. Before long we were lost causes. We sobbed and screamed, staggering helplessly, generally letting ourselves down badly. Recovery from this hysterical stage was made doubly difficult by the vision of Hill that floated before our streaming eyes. One glance and we were off again. A single eyeful of the ridiculous angle his glittering feet made in mid-prance was quite enough to reduce us to absolute physical helplessness.

And so the long day wore on.

Only afterwards did it occur to me that the innocently intended remark 'What a way to make a living' carried further implications, all of which applied to the entire rock and roll business so far as I could immediately discern. Not least music journalists (or 'rock scribes' as they were known a while ago).

If The Slade were gormless – as plainly they were – what, then, were we? Hypocrites? Mostly. Cynics? Some of us were deeply cynical and the rot was spreading. So (gulp) were we, like The Slade, gormless? I was beginning to think so. In fact, the more I examined the problem, the worse the light we all appeared in.

I am proud to say I have never looked back.

I cannot claim that the process whereby I progressed from disillusionment to outright spleen was difficult to achieve. Inevitably I tried the Dave Hill Test on other rock and roll acts. Invariably it worked on at least some levels. A few minutes' meditation on the face, body or attitudes of virtually any rock and roll celebrity was almost always sufficient to induce a paroxysm of hilarity – in which, I must add, there was always more than a trace of self-reproach. My world began to resemble a chamber of horrors, peopled by simpering babes; pompous and self-obsessed near-undergraduates; wicked financiers; frankly idiotic consumers; and, lastly, weedy hacks such as myself, guilty not only of all the above venalities, but also of suppressing any trace of intellectual honesty in favour of perpetrating our own lush, but despicable, mode of existence.

From there I turned my attention to my own former idols, for the most part now dead, living hoggishly in California, or neurotically flogging the same old cadavers up hill and, yes, down dale. I developed a new secret ruthlessness in this private demolition work which sustained me spiritually throughout the increasingly grim years of the magazine's steady climb back to commercial pre-eminence. This process was made a good deal easier by the apparent spread of comparable attitudes among some of my colleagues – yet even so I noticed that there was always a line they did not care to cross. Yes, they would allow, so and so was certainly a 'dork', and X was beyond doubt a 'nerd', and The Ums were the most witless bunch of 'bozos' ever to tread boards or cut wax. But try to nail one of their own special favourites – I soon learned who these were – and one would run into a sudden wall of reason, righteousness and irritating fair-mindedness. Other colleagues similarly betrayed promising starts with ill-timed, sentimental recidivism. No one, it seemed, apart from myself (and I was too cowardly) was willing to make the one-way trek into Renegade County.

So matters stood until I enjoyed a freakish bit of luck with a couple of books and was at last able to add courage to my convictions. I resigned from the magazine and went to live apart from the rock world. As I put it at the time – and may well have believed – I was trying to rediscover my ideals.

Which brings me, alas, to the second principal reason why this slender volume has come into being. In a word, money.

Yes, money. I haven't got any. Various high-flown writing projects having bitten the dust – deservedly in most cases – my financial position has been growing steadily more and more precarious. To be brutally precise, any moment now a knock may come on the door and my meagre store of goods will vanish into the maw of a bailiff's pantechnicon. When I first became aware of this danger I realized that what I needed was a book that would be quick and easy to write, easy to produce, and would stand a reasonable commercial chance.

I Hate Rock and Roll is it. My blueprint for security. My hope for happiness.

It is my contention that I have concealed none of my motives for writing it. They are – I'll say it again – unworthy and opportunist. That said, if you, the honoured purchaser, don't like what you find inside, it's no use accusing me of dishonesty. Besides, so long as you've actually paid for the book, I couldn't care less whether you like it or not. I don't want to be rude – not to you, anyway – but to me, languishing in financial *extremis*, you're just a blip on my Texas Instruments calculator and my only concern is which side of the decimal point you go.

However, if, after reading *I Hate Rock and Roll*, you feel that you agree with the sentiments expressed in the title – then, fine.

Welcome to my rathole.

If you should take it in mind to write me a reasoned criticism of the book, forget it. Take my advice. Abandon the project. I'll never read it. Why should I, after all?

Finally, although this is (I hope) a remote possibility, if anybody there takes the book so personally that they decide to come looking for me with a tyre iron, I strongly recommend you think twice. I live in a remote part of the countryside . . . very difficult to find . . . and as a last line of defence I've got a five-shot repeating 12-bore shotgun which I've *never yet used*, and as I've forsworn the butchery of bird and beast, only humans are left to me.

That's about it, forewordwise.

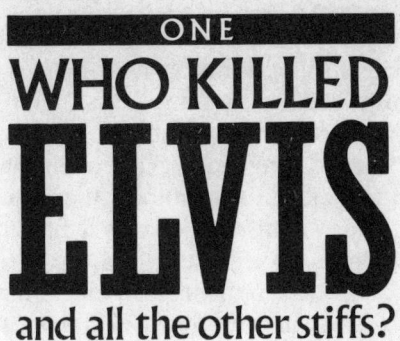

ONE
WHO KILLED
ELVIS
and all the other stiffs?

Like many another failed movement, the history of rock and roll is littered with corpses, destroyed reputations, withered hopes and tattered fantasies.

The first coherent slogan to emerge from what had hitherto been a cult but was now *ipso facto* a movement – a movement, incidentally, which has since become excessively slogan-ridden – was also one of the earliest casualties. ROCK AND ROLL WILL NEVER DIE, chanted numerous enthusiasts of the late fifties, conveniently overlooking the unwelcome yet wholly evident truth that rock and roll was expiring of old age even as the adenoidal didacticism rang sullenly for the first time around the Western world. By the closing of the decade that had given it birth, it was a memory, a golden rose of summer, a stiff.

Elvis Presley, a spent bullet though not yet a stiff, was in the United States army. Other minor luminaries were dead. One or two were in jail, or should have been, and already an entirely new wave of unpleasant adolescent crooners had sprung into being, neatly snipping off the gonads of the Founding Fathers on their way up. No matter. The redundant slogan had a certain ring to it – like ONWARD TO JERUSALEM – a good deal of money had already been invested and, most crucially of all, the inarticulate (though by no means unattractive), causelessly rebellious youth attitudes of the fifties were slipping away. The rebellion could now only stay in being if a cause could be found to sustain it. So the search immediately began for suitable candidates – as indeed it is pursued to this day, a continuous performance from which I personally derive a great deal of enjoyment – but in the meantime the slogan itself had to hold the breach.

The obvious question here is, how on earth did the early, conservative fans – and the Founding Fathers themselves – ever come to sanction such a feat of unethical cryogenics? Well, those fans who recognized what was going on had long since begun to lose interest, and besides, they'd never had a voice. That leaves the F. Fathers. What of them? What do they think of it so far?

Clearly the answer won't be coming from Elvis Presley, who, more than anyone, can be said to have started it all – though, equally obviously, he never at any stage appreciated what was happening, nor needed to, having been elected a symbol rather than a leader, prophet or guru. His monarchy was always strictly constitutional. Moreover, his rise to a kind of fame took place when the social climate, though naive and ignorant, was not so intrinsically totalitarian as that of later epochs; especially the sixties, decade of idiot messiahs. In Presley's day any singer, be he ever so popular and adored, who attempted to weave for himself the mantle of guru or (God help us) spokesman of a generation, would have been greeted with choice epithets and showers of overripe fruit.

Nevertheless, although Presley cannot help our inquiries in any direct sense, a short study of his career can provide useful insight. Actually, as I suggested earlier, it forms a kind of yardstick.

Presley began extremely well, sustained his effort for perhaps three years, then sank rapidly into an abyss so fathomless that for the next *twenty* years his efforts to extricate himself – and he didn't make too many of these – were almost entirely unsuccessful. I say *almost* because it has been suggested in some quarters that Presley did manage to extricate himself in the evening of his life. I dispute this. What we see, in Presley's seventies comeback, is not a renewed giant, a recrowned king, a reborn soul emerging radiant from the pit, but a collection of fat, heavily beringed fingers scrabbling wildly on the margins of the abyss; and what we hear, as those pudgy digits lose their hold and vanish, is no full-blooded scream of terror, but a sigh, a whimper . . . then silence.

It would have been a lot better for Presley had his rise been a good deal less dizzying, and therefore less supposedly enduring. He might never have re-established himself after his army service (it is a moot point whether he ever truly did), and as a result would have led a less unreal and more survivable life. He might even – I concede this is unlikely – have preferred to stay in the army. He might have acquired a different style of management. Any of these could have saved him. But Fate, the rotten old dyke, dealt him a bum hand. Endowing him with astonishing physical attributes, she short-changed him viciously in her apportionment of intelligence. The beautiful hulk, thus cruelly shorn of a vital means of self-defence, fell easy prey to a shadowy collection of lurkers who, though only marginally less dense than Elvis himself, possessed just that edge which enabled them to tether him to a farmyard post and milk him until his tits ran dry.

Even after the milk ceased to flow in quantity – to polish off this dismal metaphor – the stockmen refused to release the dumb beast, but carried on squeezing and fondling, kneading and working, treasuring every precious drop, storing it, serving it up again and again in dried, sterilized and reconstituted form. To encourage the animal to produce – or to console it for failing to produce – they force-fed it on a grossly over-rich diet. The animal put on weight and a few more opalescent drops trickled reluctantly into the pail. Yihaaa! Here was the formula! Working with gap-toothed rural gusto, the stockmen rapidly crammed handful after handful of protein pellets down the open throat. But now the beast grew so fat it wanted to lie down, so, as this would have compromised the flow altogether, the stockmen gave it special pills to make it lose some of the recently acquired weight. Still it pined, so they gave it yet more pills, to enable it to overlook its daily misery. When these failed to arrest the decline, they allowed it to breed. But then the selected heifer absconded with another of the beeves . . . and while the frantic stockmen were debating their next move, the beast quietly lay down and croaked.

Needless to say, the marketing of the butchered meat continues.

Quite clearly Presley himself is at least partially culpable. In the last analysis we are each of us responsible for our own actions, even those of us unlucky enough to be handicapped in some way. Presley was handicapped, as has been said, by a startling lack of nous. Additionally, his hopes of mental growth were blasted from the outset by the unfortunate combination of an overfond mother and a parochial environment. He was afflicted by exceptional bad luck in these and other things. All this mitigates his share of the blame. Yet at the same time he stands convicted of several faults. He lacked moral courage. Connected with this was Presley's inability to detect, or even seek, excellence in others – his complete unwillingness to make any attempt whatsoever to search beyond the confines of his own ruinously spoiled ego. Even later in life he made no effort to impose any checks on his immature impulses. Outwardly and celebratedly humble, he was in fact possessed of a sublime self-conceit.

Against these defects and errors, Elvis's minor aesthetic blunders – chief of these being a hideous predilection for what is piquantly termed schlock – and his supine acquiescence in a multitude of outrageous heists perpetrated on his followers throughout his entire career, can be seen to pale into insignificance.

Ah yes, the followers, the fans. What of them? Surely it may be said with perfect truthfulness that never in the field of popular entertainment has so dedicated a following been so shamefully misused. Contemptuously betrayed time and time again, they stuck to 'the King' like a species of epoxy resin – up to and, alas, beyond the grave. It is hardly worth pointing out that Elvis's fans are nonpareil in their doglike ability to suspend all critical faculties where the King is concerned. God help them, they are positively famous for it.

I am, of course, reminded of the many reports I've either read or heard first-hand from those who actually met Presley. These, when you examine them, all boil down to the same sorry story. After weeks or months, and in some cases years, of delicate negotiation, the party is informed, via intermediates, that an audience has been arranged, at Fort Presley, otherwise known as Graceland, Memphis, Tennessee, USA. A long haul if you happen to live in Slough, England – but no matter! The King has said yea! Off they go: four thousand disgusting airline miles to Memphis; get off the plane; climb into a car driven by an albino hood, drive, get out of the car, and hang around (quite different, you understand, from 'hanging out'). For hours. Meanwhile there is a continuous and audible backdrop of clicking pool balls and nasty, sycophantic laughter from a nearby room. Wait. Watch the creeps come and go. Shuffle the feet. A gaggle of creeps appears, clustered around a distant doorway – and suddenly Elvis is there, wedged in the frame, looking shorter and fatter than you expected. Shake hands. Have your picture taken by a friend. Click. Drat it – the film's jammed. That's better. Click. Say, thanks, El' – but the creeps have closed in, on receipt of an invisible signal, and the 'King' has 'split'. Pummel the old memory. What was it he actually said? He did say something. He must have done. I distinctly saw his lips move. *Nztmch*? Can't be that – sounds like Assyrian. *Nice to meet ya*? That was it. Quick, write it down. Dear Diary. Today I flew 4000 miles to be introduced to Elvis. He said it was nice to meet me. Phew! What a day! I'll never forget it.

A questioning of Elvis's *apparat* – or of Elvis himself – wasn't going to come from this quarter. If it had, he wouldn't have been allowed to hear about it. But the real trouble was, even if Elvis *had* heard about it, he wouldn't have given a toss anyway.

By the beginning of the 1970s it had long been clear to persons possessed of even half a brain that the King of rock and roll had no intention whatever of straying more than a mile from his Graceland fleshpot – unless by some chance the fee was truly astronomical.

Nevertheless, British music journals never ceased to speculate, right up to the last thunder-racked minute that he might be induced to do so. He might somehow be persuaded to make a trip to the *Royaume Uni* and so provide at last some real return to his betrayed but astonishingly loyal British fans.

Some hopeful, or perhaps excessively cynical, promoter would make known the substance of a recent offer to Presley's manager-figure, 'Colonel' Tom Parker. These offers grew steadily more fantastic as years lengthened into decades, Elvis's waistline expanded, and the tercios of British fans slowly accepted the improbability of such an event coming to pass. Eventually us Brits were promising him vast fees, our most prestigious stadia, and (some said) the services of HM the Queen to change his neckscarf halfway through the set. All these offers, realistically made or not, were doomed. Those on the job, or journals, were informed by the promoter of the breakdown of negotiations and would, with automatic reverence, pass this information to the public. This, you understand, was the procedure; by the middle seventies it had become whiskery and time-hallowed, like certain other British traditional rituals.

It was in about 1973, after a lapse of several disconsolate years, that the latest of these absurd 'offers' was made. In due course the reply – nope – was communicated to us, and the then editor set up a vigorous headline on the front cover of the magazine: ELVIS SAYS NO TO BRITAIN! I was asked to comment. I felt, and said, that this headline's truly laughable predictability barred it from so prominent a position on our cherished front cover. EARTH IN ORBIT AROUND SUN, I remember suggesting, suffered from comparable drawbacks. The point was not taken at the time but this headline never again appeared on the front cover.

In the meantime I left the journal, under circumstances explained in the Foreword, and retired to private life. Then Elvis died. I chanced to be visiting the editorial offices the day afterwards, when the magazine's approach to the tragedy was being anxiously debated. Again, and for the last time ever, I was asked for my views. I suggested that, for once, ELVIS SAYS NO TO BRITAIN would suit admirably. Might convey, as it were, a waggish yet courageous refusal to acknowledge the traditional constraints of death. This suggestion was contemptuously (and rightly) rejected. Shortly afterwards snivelling panegyrics appeared in my late organ and its rival publications. The pressure of being the King. The drugs. The lifestyle. The failed marriage. We are all guilty, *et cetera*.

Guilty? *All* of us? I never saw Elvis, never met him, never played pool with him, never paid to see any of his unspeakable films – bought one early LP, true, but I'm allowed one blunder. Elvis never gave *me* a Cadillac. As far as I'm concerned, Elvis Presley died of a drug overdose, probably induced by a subconscious desire to loosen hold on a life which had become, even for so dim a bulb as Presley, tedious and hateful – despite its legendary and repellent opulence, or because of it.

For allowing this miserable state of affairs to develop in the first place, you must blame Presley himself, his massed ranks of exploiters, and the witless legions who think of themselves as his fans. In other words, by and large the very persons who always stood to lose the most by the King joining the ranks of the snuffed.

Yes, Elvis is dead and gone, Lord, Lord. And so forth. Funnily enough we all have to go sometime – but there's no denying that Presley chose a hard road. One can only piously hope that one day, while he's up there on a cloud with a ghostly guitar in one hand and a spectral cheeseburger in the other, he'll find it worth his while to take a quick peep downwards, at the sea of shit he left behind.

The fact remains that if rock and roll ever meant anything at all – which I doubt, personally, though I'll leave that aside for now – then it meant Elvis, the poor, doomed bastard.

The first ten dreadful years threw up stars other than Presley. Not all of these, it must be admitted, are yet dead.

A few, having successfully hijacked a second ride to fame on the back of one or another of the various renaissances (by my count, three at least), have even been proclaimed stars since the true death of rock and roll. The wary, avaricious faces of these survivors make them easy to pick out in a crowd. More pertinent still is the fact that not only are they expensive to hire, but they are even more expensive to pay off in a libel settlement. Safer by far to continue concentrating on the stiffs, of whom, luckily, there is a whole 'mess'.

There are really only two major sub-groupings in the continuing catalogue of the croaked. The first comprises that vast army who have passed on to their undoubted reward as a direct result of imperfections in the science of aviation; the second consists of that even larger collection who expired as a result of ingesting hostile or unsuitable substances. (A third, much smaller, group includes those who have died in humble road accidents, or from more or less normal causes.)

One cannot contemplate the first subgroup without recalling the ghostly figure of the wartime swing bandleader, Glenn Miller; the very first showbusiness musician of note to perish in a plane crash.* Curiously enough, the second, Buddy Holly, was also distinguished from

---

* Though mystery still surrounds this event. The plane was never seen to crash; it simply disappeared. At the time of writing, a new theory is being actively promulgated: that Miller was in fact suffering from cigarette-induced lung cancer, and was spirited away to a clinic in Liberated Europe, where he subsequently died. If this should turn out to be true, then properly speaking Miller should be regarded as the founder member of our *second* group of showbiz victim figures, since nicotine is now regarded as a hostile substance, and by smoking sixty a day (as Miller did), one naturally ingests the stuff.

his contemporaries by pleasant, reedy, inoffensive music, hornrimmed spectacles, and aerial disaster. Holly was additionally notable for (a) hailing from Texas, and (b) introducing the contoured solid-bodied guitar. In his efforts to popularize the Lone Star State, Holly was clearly up against something too big for him, but in his latter branch of innovation he enjoyed a lasting success. Mention should also be made of the fact that Holly is claimed by many to have founded a separate school of rock and roll style. This, if the claim be true, can be described as a tinny production sound and a curious obsession with musical triplets. Nevertheless, his records still enjoy 'meaningful' sales (at least, such is the hope of former Beatle Paul McCartney, who in recent years acquired the entire Holly song catalogue as an investment; time will show whether the Former Fab will recoup his capital outlay).

Next on the list are two virtual nonentities – Ritchie Valens and a person with the unlikely soubriquet of Big Bopper. They are traditionally mentioned in the same reverent breath as Buddy Holly on account of the fact that they were travelling in the same plane at the same time. (One wonders, does one not, as to what name was inscribed on Big Bopper's tomb? No doubt somebody out there can enlighten me.) That being so, the next name of real moment is that of Jim Reeves.

Reeves is barely to be classed as a 'rock artiste', being indeed a fair sample of the purely 'western' wing of country and western music, itself one of the stepfathers of the vibrant new sound. Poor Jim also went to meet his Maker as a result of a plane crash. Before that, his records had sold extremely well to rock and roll fans, making not only regional and national, but international chart placings. The crash did not alter this one bit. The glutinous sentiments Reeves conveyed via a lugubrious baritone had already attracted a following consisting almost entirely of over-the-hill female shop assistants. As a class, this group is hardly notable for ice-cool restraint, and sure enough the inevitable result of Jim's passing was an immediate mushrooming of a ghastly cult, complete with pilgrimages, shrines, vows, offerings and icons. Scarcely a saint in Christendom has attracted such a following (with the possible exception of Bernadette of Lourdes, whose fans can at least hope for something tangible by way of return). To this day, grim vestiges of the Reeves cult survive. Recently there was the case of the London housewife who was so obsessed with the deceased baritone that not only did she transform her entire house into a veritable shrine, she also named her unfortunate son Jim Reeves Wellbeloved,* and crowned her devotions with a notice to quit delivered to her long-suffering husband. Reason? She was saving herself for Jim.

*Can't remember the exact surname; wouldn't print it if I could.

Doubtless delighted at his good fortune, the grieving spouse promptly hopped it, though not without first tipping off the newspapers.

Moving forward at a jump into the later sixties, we find the age-old dream of Negro emancipation in America moving steadily towards reality. A big hello at this point to soul singer Otis Redding, who, by nosediving into a frozen lake complete with an entire orchestra, proved beyond all contention that anything Whitey could contrive in the field of rock and roll aerial disaster, blacks could surpass. Here again I must digress into personal reminiscence. I was once introduced to a black musician – in Italy, this was, I again confess – who claimed to have been a member of the grim mission which set out to recover the bodies of Otis and his personal orchestra from the wrecked plane in the aforementioned frozen lake. Carried away by the intensity of his memories, the musician became emotional as the scene came back to him.

'When we done fish Otis out,' he told me, trembling, 'Ah'll sweah the man was smilin'! He done look so peaceful!' For me, these words conjured up a vivid mental picture. I saw the parka-swathed rescuers, the frozen surface of the lake, the murky, ice-cold depths . . . and, embedded mammoth-like in a vast preservative block of translucent ice, a well-dressed black corpse wearing a huge grin of amiable good fellowship. Out of sheer nervousness, I giggled. This incurred the good fellow's suspicions, which hardened into enmity and physical threats when – again from nervousness – I followed up my faux pas with a catastrophic crack about 'soul on ice'.

Enough of this. On with the list.

Actually, to date there are only a few more names. The sole 'important' aerial casualty of the seventies, rock and rollwise, of course, was Jim Croce. He was white, American, moustachioed like Emilio Zapata and moderately free – for a singer-songwriter – of the abiding contemporary sins of whimsy and/or self-pity. But one cannot leave the subject without a word of tribute for those hundreds of rock personnel who, despite these grim examples, continue to travel by air. Any suggestion that their reasons for doing so are founded in the economics of the issue and that in a contest with sanity greed will always win are, of course, most firmly to be deplored.

Air transport has not proved to be the only, or even the major, area of danger for those who make a living (that phrase again!) from rock and roll. Still higher on the list of proven idol-snuffers has been the practice of ingesting hostile materials. The first case which springs to mind – if one discounts jazz mortalities such as Charlie 'Bird' Parker – is that of the British musician Brian Jones, formerly of the Rolling Stones pop group. In this instance – uniquely so far as I am aware – the hostile substance ingested was water, gallons of it. Every drop his lungs could hold, anyway. Jones drowned ('tragically', as the music magazines would say) in a friend's swimming pool, after first having loaded himself with enough booze, pills, *et cetera*, to make it extremely likely that he sank from sheer lack of flotation, i.e. deadweight, if you'll pardon the pun.

I should now like to furnish a short poem, originally composed on the occasion of the fifth anniversary of the unfortunate guitarist's death and (vainly) intended for publication in the magazine for which I worked. Admirers of the work of Eric Jarvis Thribb, the English 'flattist' poet, will instantly recognize a poor attempt upon the style of the master.

> *Lines on the Death,*
> *Five Years Ago, of*
> *Brian Jones, Guitarist*
>
> So Brian.
> Five years
> ago this
> week you became
> a goner.
>
> (You were
> the blond one, I
> think.)
>
> Splash. Just like
> that.
> My friend Keith says
> he pushed you
> in. But I
> like to think
> you were just
> pissed
> as a skunk.

This second doleful rollcall continues with Jimi Hendrix, a black American guitarist of undeniable originality and energy, who took a fatal cocktail of booze and mandrax as a protest against the poor quality of London nightlife; female crooner Janis Joplin, whose death from broadly similar causes was maddeningly upstaged by Hendrix's slightly earlier exit; 'Mama' Cass Elliott, who choked to death on a ham sandwich, also, for some eerie reason, in a London hotel; and Jim Morrison, of the asinine Doors group, who arrived at the Pearly Gates bollock-naked and dripping wet from a bath in Paris, France. Another drug case, as is sometimes alleged. Certainly he didn't die from drowning.

The list goes on and on, and will undoubtedly be out of date by the time this book reaches print stage. Also to be included are Duane Allman, the American guitarist; Jimmy McCulloch, the pint-sized British guitarist, and Paul Kossoff, yet another British guitarist, a member of the Free pop group.

Finally – still under this drugs subheading of the hostile substances group – there is the strange case of Sid Vicious.

Sid Vicious! If ever a single career summed up all that is fatuous, malevolent and plain stupid about the great rock and roll experience, this story has got to be it.

Vicious emerged from the mid-seventies English New Wave, as it is called, like an incubus from behind an inverted crucifix at some ghastly all-England black mass. So vile were his manners, so idiotic and violent his pronouncements and behaviour – so utterly *outré* was the whole Vicious experience – that the little shit was instantly adopted by the pop media (at the time masochistically welcoming more and more incubi and succubi into their sphere of acceptance). Within days, it seemed, the most loathsome of the exciting new bands (by their own standards as well as mine), the Sex Pistols, had signed him up, although simultaneously their record company was signing *them down*, i.e. out of the front door, and pronto. No matter. Hello Sid! Join us, won't you, in our fearless fight against the Establishment, old-hat record companies, corrupt media and the human race generally! We've nothing but our pimples, our spittle, our stains and your switchblade, but we'll triumph in the end.

Sid joined – it was either them or Pol Pot, I guess – and for a few more hideous months the Sex Pistols pursued their mindless rampage. Then they fell out – how and why is unimportant – and broke up into constituent particles, two nasty little horrors this way, another nasty little horror that way – and the nastiest of all the little horrors, our Sid, across the water to New York City, where most little horrors, it seems, gravitate in the end.

From then on it was all downhill. With his girlfriend in tow he cruised the gaudier nightspots, sleeping them off at the Chelsea Hotel, famed centre of bohemianism and much else besides. This girlfriend, or 'his lady', as the jargon had it, was named Nancy. Sid took part in a couple of promotional if not exactly artistic activities – an album and a film called *The Great Rock and Roll Swindle*. From the title it initially appeared that Sid and circle were at last saying something semi-worth-while, or at least coherent. Unfortunately, both were entirely devoid of merit, being indeed notable only for their total lack of that quality (which is actually quite unusual). All the time Sid and Nancy were shoving enough heroin into their pimply bodies seriously to prejudice their continued physical health and mental stability. One night Sid got loaded and, in waking from his coma, the real, hidden Sid temporarily emerged; or perhaps (sepulchral chuckle) something *got* Sid! Know what I mean? What happened was, Sid sank his stiletto into his girlfriend enough times, and with sufficient incisive force, to occasion death. 'I was asleep, I don't remember nothing,' protested the wretched creature as New York's finest chewed sugarless gum and wrote down his version of events with the dispassionate calm of their ilk, having, you understand, seen it all before. Newspapers splashed the horrible story everywhere, and people shook their heads and muttered: 'Always said them punks would come to a bad end.' Sid, obviously in shock, was somehow bailed, on stiffish terms. Sid's mother – who appears to have played the fullest part in the development of her son's character – flew melodramatically to the Big Apple to lend her son moral support. Armed with this new sure shield, Sid went out carousing again and stabbed a harmless punter in a nightclub with a broken bottle, causing severe lacerations. Rebailed and somehow still on the loose, he was found dead a couple of mornings later, having taken an overdose of contaminated heroin. It is justifiable to say that this was the first intelligent act of his miserable life.

His mother is still on the loose, mind you.

Stunned by the ugly and grotesque manner of this unappealing anti-hero's demise, the rock and roll establishment – here temporarily defined as the hacks who had encouraged all this bilge to proliferate in the first place, feeding off the sensation and in some cases espousing some fancied social and artistic point they assumed was being established by Vicious-style behaviour – raised their hands in an almighty shout of collective horror. Not difficult. But of inquests there were none. The more fatuous writers and punters, not to mention 'acts' whose opinions were unwisely solicited, actually tried to boost the evil and dangerous Too Fast To Live/Too Young To Die theme, impertinently and inaccurately likening this sordid and murderous little loser junkie to Icarus, who flew too near the sun and perished, indirectly, from a surfeit of exaltation and God-frenzy.

In other words, although Vicious had utterly failed in everything he'd imagined he'd set out to do and had died a pathetic and gruesome loser's death – after first butchering, whether *compos mentis* or not, the only human being whose society had been less than a total disaster for him – to admit as much would have been necessarily to admit a great deal more. Participants in the wonderful rock and roll experience – punters, pundits, promoters, performers and poseurs – all conspire tacitly on occasions to conceal the truth of an unpleasant situation from themselves and each other. This is a dangerous and dishonourable neurosis. People went *very* quiet on the subject immediately after the passing of Sid, and have remained uncharacteristically reticent ever since.

Yet the deathwish motif has never gone away, is with us still, and is probably part of the overall mythos; and any idiot who kills himself within the acceptable ambit of romantic rock death can count on his faults being minimized in his public valedictories, while his puny achievements will be extolled up to and beyond the point of total absurdity. Only when honour and the rites have been satisfied, and face saved, will real evaluations of the corpse permeate quietly through, often against considerable resistance. After which he or she will either be forgotten as quickly as possible, as in Sid's case, or, as in the case of Jim Reeves, John Lennon and most of all Elvis, he will immediately find his mortal demigod status ratified by the Olympians of the Olivetti. And as far as the truth goes, that will be that for evermore.

It *is* perfectly possible to see Sid-as-victim – among other things. Had he been more of a schlemiel and less of a schmuck it might have been possible actually to feel sorry for him. But like so many others – Elvis again comes to mind – Sid was managing director and principal shareholder of his own death scene.

Irrational behaviour in human beings is not rare, but one of the built-in checks and balances our species has is its members' ability to detect the beginnings of irrationality in others, and divert or contain them before matters go too far. In the case of Sid Vicious, the circumstances of a rock and roll environment, especially if one is famous, or rich, or at least notorious, remove the weak intellect from contact with these corrective influences. (As, indeed, in the case of Elvis.) Mostly this results in nothing more serious than a spoiled ego, some expensive habits, and in the end an unlikeable personality. Often it results in neurosis. Neurosis can easily lead to tragedy.

So, bearing in mind all that is sometimes claimed for the 'alternative' way of looking at things (as promoted by the rock mythos), what can be learned? That, despite all the claims, the world of rock and roll is fully capable of as much self-deception, rather more self-satisfaction and considerably more self-righteousness than, say, big business, so frequently lambasted in scornful asides by the sixth-formers and seventh-graders who are most involved in the ongoing formulation of received rock wisdom. That no mechanisms exist within their rock philosophy for detecting and constructively dealing with the occasional aberrant type. That human nature is far more perverse than is dreamed of in their philosophy; and therefore that *any* philosophy that fails so often to live up to its boasts has no further right to be regarded with any sort of favour.

All this is a great deal to infer from a single sordid but otherwise unimportant career. But what would you? The essence of logic is that one must follow where it leads, and besides, only one other theory accounts for the strange case of Sid Vicious. It is, as I hinted earlier, that Sid actually, literally, *was* possessed, *Exorcist*-style. That a Thingy from the Outer Circle – an ab-human – took him over and made him its slave. Till death did them part (or so we hope). Three things stop me pursuing this interesting hypothesis. One, that this book has made quite enough mention of . . . you know who. Two, that any successful plot reconstruction would tend to exculpate our hero. And, three, that in order to carry it off I'd have to make myself think like Billy Graham, or one of those hellsapoppin, witch-smelling, bongo Christians from America's Deep (as in Loony) South. And on the whole – taking everything into consideration – I think I'd rather be Sid.

The final category is that devoted to road accidents and one-offs from which little or nothing may be deduced; they are included here to round the thing off, and perhaps to boost the general feeling of morbid fascination which I am trying to promote. The best known is Eddie Cochran, an early Elvis clone who had none the less the basics of an idiosyncratic style, and who ran out of luck and road in the late fifties. And how could we forget or omit Britain's very own late Marc Bolan, who had been big – 'vast' says it more truly – in Britain at around the time of The Slade, and for very similar reasons. Bolan's career had since skidded alarmingly but he stuck to it all the same. He was actually mounting a comeback of sorts when his girlfriend drove him into a tree.

The poignancy, the irony, of being snuffed thus untimely, especially when Comebacksville looms on the horizon (the deadly glow that seems to whisper: 'This way, man. That black shadow in your way isn't a tree, it's just a trick of the light. [Pause. Crunch.] Heh heh. I *hate* rockstars!'). What does the homely demise of the Boppin' Elf* remind you of? Who else that we know died on the Way Back from Wyoming, figuratively speaking? What major ex-luminary, what seminal rock figure, now dead, what famous stiff have we missed out so far?

Correct. John Ono Lennon, former Beatle. *He*, as all know, died of five gunshot wounds in late November 1980. Where does *he* fit in? How can *this* monstrous event be made to serve an anti-rock and roll purpose? Is *nothing* sacred?

In the first place Lennon is *not* entitled to a category all his own for one very good reason: his cause of death was the ingestion of a hostile substance – i.e. cupronickel and lead; and so he comes under category

* The Boppin' Elf was Bolan's popular monicker in the UK at the time. Reason enough for bad karma, you might be forgiven for thinking.

B. Nor was he the first rock star to die of a gunshot wound. Soul singer
Sam Cooke (they get around, these soul singers, don't they?) was also
bumped off by an unfriendly pistolero. The Beatles' former tour manager and oldest friend Mal Evans was plugged by the Los Angeles city
police: by mistake, of course. Lennon is but the third famous rock
person to pass on by this means, though his enormous prestige in the
rock world – second only to Elvis's or possibly Bob Dylan's – easily
outweighs the other bullet-ridden on a seniority basis. He, too, like
Elvis and Sid, needs a short dissertation.

John Lennon and the other Beatles re-enter the present work a little
later on other bases, so we must confine exegesis to deciding what can
be learned from his death. Well, for a start, Lennon was shot by a
lunatic: that much seems clear. Bad luck? Would anybody have done
as a target? Not quite. Seems the lunatic was sane enough to buy a
gun, give up his job, amass money, and come *all the way from Hawaii*
to New York with the express purpose of filling the Ironical Beatle as
full of lead as a practice castanet. Not your gibbering type of loony,
then. The plausible, Anthony Perkins type. Methodical. Resolute.
And, after the actual shocking execution, triumphant. He had no
remorse. He'd had a beef against his victim, and he'd discharged it.
Now he felt all right.

A *beef*? Not against the Sexy Beatle, the Dry Beatle, sharpest and
drollest of the Moptops, most avant-garde of the Solo Beatles, the one
who left wife, kid and (afterwards) native land – not to mention his
cutting edge – behind in order to marry an impassive but quietly
formidable (except when singing) Japanese cinéaste and sculptress,
Tokyo Rose's groovier cousin, Yoko Ono! Not against the man who
'stood for Peace', who had championed more radical causes than there
are O'Hallorans in the New York phone book, who had written pop
songs urging peace, had grown his hair and publicly palpitated his
peter for peace, who had stayed in bed for peace, marched for peace,
returned his medal for peace, been busted for peace! Who could
possibly have it in for such a seminal pillar of the alternative icono-
system? And why?

Funny you should ask that, because it turns out that the seeds of the
Lennon-slaying idea appear to have been planted by poor old John
Lennon himself, years before, in 1965, when the Outspoken Beatle
had perfectly correctly but unwisely stated the simple truth that, in
most of the Western world, the Beatles were a more significant totem
in the lives of the young than Jesus Christ.

This incident and its ramifications are famous. Throughout the
Bible-punching Deep South the drums began to beat. Vast bonfires
were lit. Tiny tots, their eyes agleam, cast their copies of Beatle
product into the blaze under the helpful aegis of snake-hipped local

radio station proprietors anxious to acquire the Moral Majority listenership. Death threats were made. Congressmen gave florid speeches. Lennon, frightened by the furore, and sincerely anxious to withdraw with some dignity, tried as hard as he could to eat his words. Most people settled for the humiliation of the climbdown. Others, among them Mark David Chapman, did not.

The slaying of John Lennon was essentially an outraged and barmy Christian's righteous slaying of the infidel, the heretic, the Antichrist; no matter what other barminesses clouded or shaped Chapman's semblance of a motive, the punishing of Lennon for an old crassness of speech was his main intent.

It's a thorn in the red rose of success, all right – the thought that the higher you go, the more necessarily famous you become; and that the more well known you are, the more danger you're in from nuts, kidnappers, drunken bigtimers in bars, and so forth. At the time of writing, the media have tenuous hold of a story that the Hell's Angels motorcycle cultists of the United States have what is called an 'open contract' on Mick Jagger, leader of the Rolling Stones. Now, it seems that just by saying too much, you actually add to these standing risks, especially if you choose to live, as Lennon did, in a large American city. Once again we see the rock lifestyle failing to equip its subscribers with any mechanism for detecting the approach of dangerous loonies or other undesirable human aberrants. Nor does it offer training to deal with danger. Witness the Rolling Stones' callow bewilderment at the Altamont festival when they found their aggressive lyrics actually coming to life right under their noses. (I was there, and remember feeling contempt for Jagger's repeated bleats of 'Cool it, willya,' his voice sounding nasal and scared and – worst of all, for a Rolling Stone – uncertain.) And yet Lennon – whose well-known espoused cause was immediate disarmament on a love-thy-neighbour basis, and who was in fact a man who wielded what can only be called political clout, since disarmament was and is a political issue of the very hottest order – was proven quite wrong in his basic assumptions about human nature in the cruellest and most terminal way. By being quite unable to protect or defend himself, he was cut off in his prime. War is over if you want it, all you need is love, give peace a chance, and love thy neighbour. Until he puts five rounds of .32 calibre into your vest.

Two important lessons here for famous rock persons:

(1) Keep your lip buttoned; you never know who you're offending, or how long he's prepared to wait.

(2) Hire a bodyguard from a reputable security firm. Stay with him. A great life at the top, right?

*   *   *

But I do not wish to close on such a sour and brooding note. Death is not all bad, nor are all deaths irredeemably portentous.

Of all the names mentioned, oddly enough the one which for me stands out is that of 'Mama' Cass Elliott, who, remember, choked to death on a ham sandwich while living in a London hotel. And the reason is her uniquely homely and almost lighthearted way of passing on. She was the physical opposite of Karen Carpenter, who died of anorexic complications in 1983. Cass Elliott was a large girl. Not so fat as some you see, but definitely on the substantial side. Had she been thin there would have been no tragicomic side to her demise. But she didn't *need* the ham sandwich. She merely wanted it. And so she died.

Face it, you have to be something of a plutocrat to log enough airline miles to make you a statistically probable casualty of the airline system; similarly you have to be quite rich, at least in potential, to work up a decent addiction to a Class A drug. In all but a few cases where an overdose or lethal macedoine of drugs brings death, few can claim that death has resulted from ignorance. Carelessness, yes. Contempt. Self-contempt. Here are your real killers, not the chemicals. Yet the drugs each carry their own special penalties and peculiarities. The ability to recognize and respect these is what distinguishes the bold experimenter from the stiffening cadaver on the hotel bed. Of course it is sad, but it is also usually stupid, or in rare cases deliberate, and also seems, with hindsight, to have been inevitable at least half the time. The event is thus robbed of sympathy.

I feel far sorrier for vivisected animals than for hardened junkies who get it wrong and end up in the morgue with labels on their big toes. Hardened junkies should know their business, their 'scene'. When a bomb-carrying psychopath blows it – literally – and ends up across fifty yards of olive-drab railings, we tend to fancy a spot of poetic justice has taken place. Junkies are not to be compared with terrorists, but the culpability laws apply just as rigidly.

As for car crashes, nothing whatever can be deduced. I myself have been in several.

But to choke to death on . . . a ham sandwich! Here, surely, is true greatness, true originality! Truly 'nothing in her life became her like her manner of leaving it'. Why, it could happen to me! Better still, it could happen to you! No plutocracy here. It is a death within reach of all but the very humblest, on a par with being knocked down by a bus or electrocuted by a toaster.

Its humility stimulates sympathy.

How many of these other deaths do the same? None, in my view.

Let us therefore move on to the Quick.

TWO

LOOK AT ME
I'M STUPID

from the ridiculous to the ridiculous

At about the time that psychedelia was taking off on a grand scale in most major Western capitals, I was in Athens. The year was 1967.

The Colonels had just taken over. Tanks crouched on street corners. Everywhere was the whiff of oppression – the kind of tangible odour one imagines producing the same effect on a card-carrying member of Amnesty International as the fumes of *allium sativum* are said to do on Count Dracula and other beings of the night.

What better time and place to try out one's newly acquired hippie gear?

Item: one lurid kingfisher kaftan in Chinese fake silk, embroidered with scenes of Manchu executions. Item: one pair of – if you can believe this – gold lamé trousers, ludicrously flared. Item: one necklace of white plastic monkey skulls, graded according to size, like pearls of the South Sea.

As I eagerly donned this vile *mélange*, warning visions flashed before my eyes. I saw again the ill-concealed incredulity of the Rome tailor as the commission was explained to him in detail; I saw the doubtful, sly grins exchanged by other members of the band as I displayed my new wardrobe to them before packing for the journey to Athens and the one-month residency in the Hilton (it was that kind of band). I ignored the omens and continued dressing.

Evening came down like a jackboot. The hotel doorman recoiled in terror as the glorious apparition that was *moi* wafted past him and out into the gloaming. The fumes of the Levant had addled my brain. Filled with a fierce and un-British lust to promenade in my new ensemble, I set course for the city lights, a beatific smile on my face, the monkey skulls swinging together with a satisfying clunk just south of my chin.

To this day I cannot recall with any clarity what it was I believed at that time; what the hippie ideal meant to me personally. I seem to remember it had something to do with the idea that, by posing in bright garments, I might somehow bring peace and enlightenment upon whomsoever entered my numinescent orbit. I think I really did believe this. I should also explain at this point that the psychedelic extravaganza of the middle and late sixties undoubtedly lost whatever coherence it may once have possessed in direct proportion to the miles travelled in an easterly direction. By the time 'Flower Power' had reached continental Europe, where I was working at the time, it had been almost entirely stripped of any philosophical rationale, having been translated into little more than a grand costume party for the rich and bourgeois, with vague hints of benevolent aftereffects thrown in to appease former university students. The movement had overtaken me in Italy (again), where sooner or later every movement, whether religous, political or *foclorico*, becomes an excuse for dressing up. What blame, therefore, attaches to me if my version of hippiedom initially reflected the influences of my geographical location?

I had as yet had no opportunity of sampling public attitudes to my exciting new garments, though I *had* discovered the eternal truth that tolerance for Western libertarian attitudes across the board decreases proportionately as one journeys towards the rising sun (starting, of course, from California). So I was prepared, in this famous but sadly rundown former capital city of the Mediterranean world, for turned heads, rude staring and the occasional caustic remark. I did not care in the slightest. Love would conquer all.

The Bulgar – as I always think of him, and indeed he may have been one – spotted me from across the street. Like a cruising shark that has just sighted a film extra, he changed course 180 degrees and took up a position about twenty yards in my wake. Twenty minutes later he was still there, and the streets were more thinly peopled. Thinking he might be some kind of policeman in mufti, I halted in a shop doorway to allow him to make his pitch, or whatever. And indeed, he came up to me, eyes aglow.

I can only give you my word that his intentions, so apparent now, were altogether hidden from my psychedelic sight at the time. Intent on exuding an air of spiritual calm – the yin to the yang of my sartorial brilliance, you understand – I had entirely failed to appreciate the weakness of another's flesh.

He laid a grimy hand on my exotic sleeve, the black fingernails in shabby contrast to the magnificence of the woven execution scene on my cuff. Confidingly, he said, 'I tink you very fine.' Then he smiled, a ghastly seducer's leer. With horrifying suddenness the black absurdity of my position came home to me. Seeking, in my hippie innocence, to bring a little light into the totalitarian gloom of this exceptionally unprepossessing city, I had succeeded only in attracting the unwelcome attentions of a down-at-heel pederast, probably of Bulgarian extraction. I must say at once that who does what, which way up, and to whom, has never greatly troubled me. Who, you might think, am I to deny some old Bulgar a little harmless bit on the side? Indeed, I am the last person who would wish to do so, provided always that it is not I whom the Bulgar wishes to bugger. I have even heard, from certain long-preserved folk sayings, that Bulgars are positively famous for it – that the two words are etymologically linked *ipso facto*. At the time, however, I was in an awkward predicament, not wishing to be buggered by anyone.

But what could I say? Clearly the fellow thought he was responding to an attraction already broadcast by my gaudy self with intent. Bright clothes meant, to him, the vestments of somebody who wished to be buggered.

Nevertheless I tried my usual, diffident gambit of the urbane smile and the murmur of 'Sorry, not my scene, man.' His eyes lit up at my voice – God knows what he thought I'd said. He then pressed his shabby suit further, grinning with anticipation, and using graphic fore-arm movements to get his point across. He began to throb in an embarrassing way. There could be no doubt of his desires.

Nor of mine. I acted. Like a brightly coloured fireball, I shot out of the doorway, brushing past the Bulgar, and tore up the street. Humiliated by the failure of my peace-and-love costume's intended effect on the Athenians, and embarrassed at this undignified adjustment to my leisurely promenade, I nevertheless retained enough nous to appreciate that the fellow might come to prove difficult once my refusal to be buggered had been made clear to him. I burned up the street, in the direction, I hoped, of my hotel, only slowing down when it became apparent that he was not following.

This was the wrong way. Never mind. Make a left here, and here, and keep on up. Odd, it seemed as if I had just passed this way. God, I *had* just passed this way. There was the shop doorway where the Bulgar cornered me. And – Jesus Christ – there was the *Bulgar* slouching against the shutter with a sour expression. I must have come round in a complete circle.

Keep going, don't look at him. Without thinking, I broke into a jog, the monkey skulls thumping against my kingfisher chest. *Don't look at the bastard!* Too late. Unable to resist, I shot him an oblique glance which, when I saw he'd caught it, was transformed into an inane leer out of sheer terror. It must have looked utterly unequivocal. One minute the transvestite had been mincing about obviously looking for a pick-up, next minute the coquettish thing had fled, now here he came again, grinning invitingly and loping along at a catchable pace.

Grinning with joy, the bulky Bulgar broke into a trot, his barrel chest coping easily with the toil of the uphill run, while my own lungs were already bursting with nervous effort and panic. Jesus, let the hotel be where it was half an hour ago. Bliss! O joy! There it is!

With a final burst I shot up the steps and through the revolving door. So ended my attempt to convert the City of Pericles and Pappadopoulos to the Power of Flowers.

Around four o'clock the Bulgar gave up and went home. For another week this baffled and bitter Romeo hung around, never daring to pass the portals but in every other way making his presence obvious. My colleagues took to perpetrating unkind jokes; on one terrible occasion two of them actually tipped off the lurking Bulgar as to my whereabouts. This resulted in a short, embarrassing scene and the exchange of harsh words.

I never again wore the golden flares. The Manchu kaftan was eventually stolen by a waiter in Rimini, while the monkey skull necklace disappeared under baffling circumstances in Bologna.

This dreadful experience set in motion a chain of ideas which have contributed much to my present attitude towards dressing up in the name of rock and roll. This attitude may be summarized thus:

Although rock and roll performers – and followers – clearly believe that in their excesses of style they are appearing in a powerful light, i.e. chic, knowledgeable, menacing, in reality they almost always end up looking total pillocks. This may be a sad reflection on them but for the rest of us it provides a few laughs – and for someone nursing attitudes like mine and wishing to incorporate them into a diatribe, it is a positive godsend.

Mind you, such has quite often been the desired effect, the result of a deliberate if cynical choice on the part of those who control the artiste. Examples abound. Back in the late fifties there was the sixteen-year-old Scot Jackie Dennis, who incidentally can claim to be the forerunner of all British acts ever to make anything like a splash in US pop music circles. However, what was ludicrously different about Dennis was not his nationality, nor his age (Laurie London, a contemporary, was even younger, and vastly more successful), but the fact that someone had talked the poor little twerp into appearing on stage dressed in a kilt.

Now even professional Jocks will admit, under pressure, that there is something innately ridiculous about kilts. To see (for example) Prince Charles stooging about in one (if I may here borrow a great writer's most famous metaphor) is to alter one's entire concept of Man as Nature's Last Word.

Also, for an artiste to become a genuine style-setter in his own right, there must exist at least a slender chance that the fans will be persuaded to dress in a similar way – many later successes continue to be founded on this and *no other* basis. I don't mean to be unkind, but who, saving a lack-brained Pictish dolt, could possibly have believed that US youth, then discovering the dubious delights of denim, would be persuaded to abandon jeans in favour of kilts? Nobody, of course – and indeed Dennis's burst of stardom was conclusively short-lived, despite a last-minute, despairing switch to trews (tartan pants).

Seeking examples of *successful* pillockry, we move closer to our own times. Back in the early seventies, perhaps the grimmest wasteland the rock and roll cavalcade has yet traversed, the British obsession with clothes and accessories reached a new, fervid peak. How else can the otherwise inexplicable success of, say, Gary Glitter be understood? An amiable but sadly over-age and consistently overweight person, Glitter, by dressing his band in cut-price silver lamé, covering his garb with Christmas Tree dust and changing his name (from Paul Raven), scored the success the inner Gary must have long despaired of finding. Or The Slade who, though they possessed an exceptionally powerful vocalist, only achieved fame when they swopped their skinhead look (cropped hair, workaday denim clothes, large and menacing boots) *literally overnight* for a bizarre range of apparel deliberately and simultaneously evocative of the circus and extreme soccer fandom?* Or Marc Bolan, of T. Rex, another artiste who, in about his fifth entirely different visible incarnation, despite being afflicted by the presence of an extremely poor backing band – in which Bolan himself was by far the best musician (this says it all) – nevertheless made it up the ladder as far as rung two by means of the timely application of eye-liner and the inevitable glitter dust.

At the same time other artistes on the British scene, desirous of making their own mark, felt obliged to make some sort of concession towards the current obsession with clothing. David Bowie, a man of considerable though frequently overstated talent (principally as a *mimique*), then also in his sixth or seventh incarnation, took off in a big way by outdoing absolutely all the competition in this matter of bizarre, fantasy outfits. His musical output, then at a peak of originality (if you like that sort of thing), began to decline as he explored every last tedious facet of the persona the music press kept telling him he'd created thereby. Bowie, therefore, was in a sense a delayed-action victim of the clothing trap. Unlike Jackie Dennis, who appeared completely stupid to just about everybody, Bowie managed to convince a fair slice of the juvenile population, and many writers on distinguished national newspapers, that stupid was precisely what he was not. He then proceeded to prove that he was, after all, moderately dim, by

*For a detailed description of a member of The Slade, see Foreword.

allowing himself to be sidetracked into the said self-indulgent side alley.

An even more striking example remains to be brought forward. It is also one of the most subtle, and so most interesting cases.

I refer, of course, to the Case of Bryan Ferry and the Gaucho Outfit.

This celebrated affair remains one of my fondest memories. Bryan Ferry, as many will be aware, is/was/is the lead vocalist and principal songwriter – indeed, the undisputed founder figure – of another popular British combo which first achieved prominence in the early seventies, The Roxy Music. It must be said that to some extent their success was indeed due to the sounds they made, on record and, to a lesser extent at first, on stage. Ferry, by far the dominant figure, has enjoyed considerable riches and kudos as a songwriter, and indeed his quavery, precarious crooner's whinge is ideally suited to the complicated lyrics and simple melodies in which he specializes.

At the same time, it cannot be denied that a very great part of the success of The Roxy Music in general and Bryan Ferry in particular has been due to the sartorial component in their image. Indeed, this has always been consciously promoted. Ferry has clearly envisioned himself as a man of fashion in the classic, Brummelian sense. Nobody would deny that this man has a deep and sincere commitment to masculine elegance. Often, he pitches it just right. Sometimes, and joyously from my point of view, he gets it wrong – and on the occasion to which I shall shortly refer, made so spectacular a pratfall that the reverberations rang for weeks afterwards.

The first hint of the way the wind was blowing came about as a result of the *Country Life* affair. The Roxy Music released an album with this title in about 1974, and, inevitably, promotional interviews with Bryan Ferry followed. For each of these he posed for photographs wearing a beautiful Harris Tweed blazer, elegant trousers, and Bond Street boots. 'Country Life' – geddit? Now, there is nothing wrong in an artiste pursuing a promotional theme in this way but there was something about the finished photographs which caught my attention. For a moment, studying them, I couldn't make out what it was; then it dawned. I carried the pictures, and my conclusions, to other members of the magazine's staff. All agreed that the photos alone gave the impression that what was being advertised was not a Man, nor an Intellect, nor even an Album, but a Sports Jacket.

We headlined an accompanying article in a correspondingly ironical manner;* and for a few weeks there was a noticeable coolness between the magazine and the Ferry camp. As hints go, it was the gentlest

*'Achieve the Country Life look in a Cumfitwede blazer. By Ferrari of South Kensington.'

possible, but Ferry would not be deflected from his headlong dash towards disaster. If a bunch of seedy hacks (his opinion of us, and not too wide of the mark either) had the temerity to poke fun at his sartorial ambitions, why then, he'd double the stakes and be demmed! A few months afterwards The Roxy Music, then at the height of their prestige, made a long-awaited series of concert appearances. The premiere was, I think, at the Hammersmith Odeon, in London. Naturally we sent a photographer and reporter. What they brought back was gold, pure gold.

And once again a single picture told the whole sorry story. For Ferry, with an admirable determination to demonstrate that he had no intention of being cowed into submission over this matter of dress, had gone wildly over the top.

I mean, why else would a man of fashion dress up as Zorro?

What we beheld, in this superb and unprecedented series of photographs, was the complete Spanish-American ensemble. The bolero jacket. The cummerbund. The high-waisted pants. The high-heeled boots. The funny cylindrical hat with the flat brim, canted at what was presumably intended to be a rakish angle over one eye. . . . Moreover the photographer, on whom be blessings for evermore, had contrived to catch Ferry awkwardly descending a rickety staircase, eyes wide with alarm, posture contorted in an undignified way. Furthermore, he had used a flashgun, which is almost always grossly unflattering.

The results were magnificently farcical* – the humour of the situation, from our point of view, being greatly increased when one recalled how tetchy Ferry had been in his dealings with our journal. His customary feeling – that he was being got at – by no means true at the beginning of his career, became something of a self-fulfilling prophecy as writer after writer came back from interview after interview with tales of cold Ferry asides about previous treatment meted out to him; with the inevitable result that, much as we might admire the man's talent, we also undeniably began to mark him down to a certain degree on account of his sniffy and ungracious attitude.

It would have taken sterner flesh than ours to resist the God-given opportunity which now fell into our laps.

The article was routine and competent. What was needed was a snappy headline to set the thing alight.

HIDALGO HERBERT? DON DORK? EL PRATTO? Nothing I personally

---

* In fact, Ferry-as-Zorro inspired the genesis of a long-running *New Musical Express* cartoon strip character, Tony Benyon's 'Lone Groover'. The Groover, who shortly afterwards developed into a spoof on the Lone Ranger, first appeared in the issue immediately following the gaucho episode, and was a direct reaction to The Roxy Music's leader's ill-starred foray into *High Chaparral* country.

could contrive seemed worthy of such splendid fatuousness. I passed
the whole problem over to a colleague who, with truly heroic inspiration, gave us HOW GAUCHE CAN A GAUCHO GET? Stunned by his inven-
tiveness, we begged him to complete the layout with big picture
displays. The result was on an estimated 200,000 breakfast tables two
days later. An actual readership, estimated, on the dentist's-waiting-
room theory, of a cool million and a half, read the article, sniggered
at the headline, cackled wildly at the photograph.

Ferry never forgave us. Nor – and this may well be pure coincidence
– did his career continue its exponential upward climb. This is not to
say he sank like a stone; indeed, both Bryan Ferry and a version of
The Roxy Music are still with us. But – and this may only be my fancy
– something went out of him immediately after the gaucho episode.
His unhappy gaffe over the question of stagewear coincided with the
peaking of independent aspirations by other members of The Roxy
Music. The group broke up a year or two later – only to re-form,
another year or two after that, sadder but wiser men. Separately, as
is so often the case, they had failed to add up to the sum of their parts.
Ferry and The Roxy Music are now institutions, which is to say they
appear to live quite handsomely without working on anything terribly
new. And Ferry, be it noticed, sticks to lounge suits.

My point is this. Far from wishing to appear ridiculous in order to
attract attention, Ferry had always consciously wished to appear *stylish*.
And so he had – for a while. Then he overreached himself and
appeared at least temporarily more ridiculous than he can ever have
envisaged in his wildest nightmares. He is not therefore to be compared
with those who always *by design* appear ridiculous, or with his own
former colleague Brian Eno, who began by trying to appear super-
modish, then changed back in the very nick of time to a non-ridiculous
sartorial approach (while remaining wildly ridiculous in various other
ways). Bryan Ferry is therefore living proof of how even momentary
ridiculousness can spoil your swing.

The important thing, it seems to me, is to recognize that you have
strayed into ridiculousness and so come to profit from the experience.
Clearly both Bowie and Ferry have done this; each man now looks to
Fifty Shilling Tailors rather than Interplanetary Fashions Inc. for
inspiration. Jackie Dennis presumably realized too late, and so failed
to profit – but on the other hand Gary Glitter never at any time
laboured under illusions of dignity. What's more, he made an attempt
to get out of the business as soon as he decently could; though sad to
say the attempt failed and nowadays Gary still plods the circuits and
makes occasional records. Marks for seeing the light, though – and full
marks to Alice Cooper, whose entire stage act was perhaps the most
ridiculous of all (in a *Grand Guignol* sense), but who took off like a

polecat the minute his investments began to pay more than his concert tours, and has never been heard of since.

But what about the chump who never realizes at all how ridiculous he or she is? When the aspect of his appearance or act or personality which inspires healthy derision lies outside his own focus? For example, when he is short?

The entire front line of the Blue Öyster Cult is very short.

It's an odd thing when you come to think of it. Here we have a group whose musical themes are relentlessly masculine, phallic and powerful (one of their most famous numbers is called *Me 262* after the Second World War German jet fighter). The highlight of their act is when all five, clad in leather and wearing guitars, stand side by side like tiny stormtroopers, legs braced, and spray the bemused punters with synchronized electronic invective. And yet all five are so conspicuously restricted in growth that they are commonly known, among the more cynical hacks, you understand, as 'Happy', 'Dozy', 'Barmy', 'Turgid' and 'Stupid', the Five Dwarves of Heavy Metal.

Of course, some might well think – with justice – that to play Heavy Metal at all, let alone dress up in leatherwear to do so, is ludicrous enough; yet it is undeniable that the physical shortness of the Öysters (if I may so call them), when contrasted with the male-oriented fixations of their image, sound quality and lyric themes, produces an overall effect which is magnificently laughable. One of my own former colleagues on the journal, a great fan of this group and himself exceedingly short, went to interview them and came back radiant with pleasure. *All five of his interviewees had been shorter than him!* For the first time in his career he'd towered over the celebrities whose utterances he'd been sent to report. This produced a dramatic change in his attitude. Overnight, zeal became indifference, admiration turned to contempt. How must it be for the simple punter who knows the Öysters only as an audible entity, who goes in happy expectation to one of their concerts – then stares in disbelief as five menacing midgets stalk moodily from the wings, don enormous guitars whose dimensions only serve to underscore their own, and then launch into machismo motifs at high volume?

Bill Haley was ridiculous. With his large body, silly kisscurl, and extremely ill-fitting stage suits, he was perhaps the first rock and roll celebrity to inspire both admiration and derision at the same time. Eventually the admiration began to fade, as other luminaries hove into sight, but the ridiculousness remained. Haley's career never entirely expired – the man himself expired in the late seventies – but before the fifties were out he had lost whatever brief initiative he had once possessed. In the sixties and early seventies, looking exactly the same as he had in 1956, he was haunting the nostalgia circuits of the world, still pushing the same old material in his bull baritone, still exhorting his string bassist to shin up his viol in mid-tune like a monkey on a stick. Yet why should he have called it a day before he had to? Haley's was a name to conjure with, a name of legend. In his later career he undoubtedly made more money than ever he did in his brief heyday – even allowing for inflation – but as a result was doomed, like *Der Fliegender Holländer*, to sail the same old seas for eternity. Or so it seemed before kindly Death supervened. Nothing must be allowed to change if you work the nostalgia circuit. So the string bassist was still under orders to ascend his bass, the tenor saxophonist – poor, rheumatic old devil! – still had to lie on his back to play, at preordained moments. The whole cobwebbed apparatus was somehow kept in being (including the cross-eyed lead guitarist), with the result that the earlier, innate ridiculousness later became compounded by a new and entirely different form of absurdity, less easy to laugh off.

Sleep well, Bill. You're better off out of it, chum.

Then we have those rare but ineffably rewarding instances when an artiste is made to look a total pillock as a direct result of public misfortune. Frank Zappa, the distinguished American composer and musician (incidentally also a man with sound views on rock and roll), was once assaulted on the stage of London's Albert Hall and fell into an orchestra pit, breaking bones in the process. Nobody I know found this ridiculous, because Zappa's views and attitudes are widely known (if less widely understood), and he has never expressed physical truculence or any desire to confront it. Now, had something of the sort happened to the late John Bonham of Led Zeppelin – a violent and brutal individual – or to the unspeakable Ted Nugent – a real bonehead who does everything he possibly can to promote an image of himself as a red-blooded all-American killer – any resulting injury would also have had a element of absurdity, robbing the victim of sympathy.

Indeed – though this should not be interpreted as incitement – my guess is that anybody who dotted Nugent on the nose, drawing blood and exacting humiliation before thousands, and got away alive would be venerated as a folk hero and could in all probability write his own recording contract.

However, the incident I have in mind involves nothing so strenuous or violent. It is 'The Day Steve Harley Walked On Water'.

For the benefit of American – and some UK – readers, I ought to explain who Steve Harley is. It won't take long. Harley is a British singer and songwriter who first appeared on the heels of the Bowie boom, as frontman and general proprietor of a pretentious combo called Cockney Rebel. Actually not without talent, particularly as a lyricist, Harley rapidly alienated the entire music press establishment by proving almost impossible to like. His opinion of himself was clearly so elevated that one wondered why he bothered to go through the approval-soliciting process at all. 'Big-headed' is the term which springs to mind. OK, that by itself is no sin in the world of rock and roll. Harley's error was to imagine that he could somehow bypass the conventions whereby even the most conceited of stars avoids excessive self-praise like the Black Death, leaving all that sort of thing to the reporters in the name of modesty. His uncompromising refusal to abide by this gentlemanly convention, compounded by his bitter truculence towards those who attempted to interview him, certainly cleared him of any charges of hypocrisy but at the same time offended those very persons in whose ink-stained hands lay the fate of many aspirant celebrities.

Gradually the exchanges between Harley and the press revealed an almost unbridgeable gulf. At the same time the emerging star made a bold attempt to outflank the music press altogether, by ignoring them and appealing directly to the vast hosts he imagined were firmly on his side.

At this stage his career was far from unsuccessful – as recognized by the promoters of a regular one-day open-air London summer pop concert at Crystal Palace, who invited Harley to fill a prominent slot on the bill of fare. I should explain, for the benefit of those who've never been there, that Crystal Palace means, to British rock and roll fans, a spacious if rundown estate in deepest south London, with a deep dell amidmost, in the centre of which is a charming cupola'd stage moated by a small lake. Harley – what a showman – hit upon the idea of using this lake to turn the tables for ever on those who'd accused him of being big-headed. He'd actually walk on water! To this end his coolies toiled in secret to construct a platform which would lie an inch or two underneath the surface. At the climax of his act – I like to think of Harley gloating over the prospect in advance – he would step, nay, *leap* down on to this hidden platform and . . . make like JC! What admiring laughter there would be! How his stock would rise!

Of course, it went wrong – not, as some of you are doubtless hoping, because the platform collapsed under his weight, or was removed by ill-wishers in advance, but in a more subtle, if anticlimactic way.

It is a fact – as Harley should have known, or been told – that on these occasions a few punters can always be found who will of their own volition enter the Crystal Palace lake from the audience end and splash about, having fun, like the birdbrains who thrash around in the Trafalgar Square fountains in freezing weather solely because it is New Year's Eve. Of course, it happened again, pretty early in the day, despite the unavailing efforts of Harley's goons. These exhibitionists, to their delight, soon discovered the hidden platform, and before noon was high the lake was covered with strolling couples, solo wanderers, even (as I was told) a man selling hamburgers from a barrow.

So what happened? Did Harley cut his losses and abandon the walking on water scheme? Or did he inflexibly pursue the grand design right up to the final, bitterly absurd anticlimax? I wasn't actually present on this occasion and my sources do not agree as to the outcome. But it is not strictly important. What *is* certain is that faulty intelligence work, plus a little bad luck, made this man Harley look a total chump at precisely the time when, due largely to his own past pronouncements, he needed above all to convince the British rock and roll public that a chump was what he was not. Yet once the Crystal Palace audience had discovered the hidden platform – as they were bound to do – Harley was in a trap from which there could be no real escape. Nor did he escape. The effect on his career has apparently proved even more deadly than the effect of the gaucho episode on Bryan Ferry. He still makes well-engineered records, still gives the occasional bellicose and self-justifying interview . . . and has never since looked to possess more than a rank outsider's chance at the glittering peaks for which he once so boldly aimed. Too bad.

A great many black vocal combos are ridiculous.

Not (I hasten to add) because they are black, and not usually because of what they sound like, but because of what they *do* in the process of putting their material across to a live audience.

Why black combos, and especially American black combos in linear descent from the Impressions by way of Detroit, Philadelphia and, latterly, the disco capital of New York, feel such an obvious need to go in for onstage choreography has always been beyond me. There is something terribly old-fashioned about it; a whiff of the days of vaudeville, when any singer who hoped to make a living had to dance as well, and tell jokes, and most likely double on some musical instrument. Of course, it is perfectly acceptable for a vocalist or group of singers to colour a delivery by means of the occasional beautifully understated gesture and even more infrequent balletics. And so the Impressions, back in the fifties, managed things. But to carry the process to its current absurd levels, whereby of their own free will sane human beings do their sincere best to impersonate demented automata, to my mind qualifies for the perjoration 'ridiculous'.

I wouldn't mind so much if the dance routines such groups habitually employ bore any relation to the subject matter of the songs they habitually sing (this, granted, would be difficult enough in view of the extremely limited vocabulary at the disposal of disco lyric writers). But they don't.

First, absorb these lyrics.

> Gonna tell you 'bout a thing called LURVE.
> That's L-O-V-E LURVE
> It's with you all the DAY (oo-wee)
> It's with you in every WAY (all right)
>   Get down 'n party, etc.

OK, nobody expects *King Lear* on such occasions but you'll have to agree the sentiments don't exactly set you on fire. No matter, you say – I've heard worse. And indeed you almost certainly have. The point is, the group (name forgotten) heard delivering this number accompanied these trite nothings with the most astounding and dedicated display of meaningless athletics I've ever witnessed.

Gonna tell you 'bout a thing called LURVE was dished up accompanied by a frantic scissoring of the knees and swift alternate glances to stage left and stage right. *LURVE* (1st time) was followed by a dextrous double pirouette, the two left-hand men spinning widdershins, the two right-hand men turning clockwise. At *L-O-V-E LURVE* the ensemble began to mark time, stiffly, like majorettes with piles; on *DAY* they executed another double pirouette and re-formed in two rows facing each other. And for the final line the soloist sprang forward and did a handstand that would have been a credit to an eleven-year-old Rumanian androgyne, while at the same time the other three pirouetted yet again three times, went clap-clap-clap in double tempo, and did the splits.

The timing was precise, the athleticism astonishing, the dedication wholly impressive, the effect foolish in the extreme.

For a start nobody was looking (except me, but I don't dance). Secondly, the lack of any association between words and movement made both seem vapid. Thirdly, the overall subordination of the performers' individual identities to the grim mechanics of the Routine was distasteful and reactionary.

Of course, the theory is that, by jigging about in a synchronized way throughout a tune, the artiste transmits to the onlookers a burning and passionate desire to 'boogie', 'party' and otherwise 'get down'. And it is perfectly true that a very good way of getting an audience to dance – and therefore into a happy state of tolerance for lyrics that, for all they know, have been written by a pocket calculator – is for the performer himself to dance. The catch is, of course, that if everybody is dancing who is looking at the band? And if nobody's looking – the object presumably being achieved – then why are the band still jigging about? The other side of the same coin is that if the group are performing in a place where dancing, or even partying, is not permitted, say a concert theatre, the resulting juxtaposition of partying performers and placid punters creates a droll effect. The activity gulf (if so I may describe it) between performers and performed-to must not be too wide, or the former will simply fail to carry the latter with them. The punters might like to come along but the rules don't permit. So they will always *seem* to be sitting on their hands and the group will always *seem* to be trying too hard. Here is a situation fraught with potential ridiculousness.

Of course, I could go on. And I will, for just a while longer.

When you come to consider it, not only are there a great many ways in which an artiste or whole act can make themselves look absurd, but each category has a large and growing membership.

The first category we examined was that of absurd clothing. Victims of this particular trap include David Bowie, Bryan Ferry, and the long-lost Jackie Dennis. Wearers of *deliberately* absurd clothing, however, like Alice Cooper, Screamin' Jay Hawkins and Gary Glitter, are exculpated. Indeed, they benefited. And they have their descendants.

Many other names of clothing trap victims will occur to readers. For starters, and as a line for future research, I give you (a) all the cartridge-belted, leather-jacketed, long-haired, toothless survivors of the Jurassic Heavy Metal era; (b) all recidivist Teds; (c) punk rockers, then and especially now; (d) New Romantics; (e) anybody with a Mohawk haircut; and (f) Boy George. Mind you, I have a feeling that the last-named may yet follow in the footsteps of those who saw the jaws of the trap closing and made a bid for freedom before it was too late. Boy's style of transsexual poseurie is so extreme and overdone that I rather suspect he's softening up his many followers for a sudden, death-defying switch to short hair, stubble and lounge suits. Like Mick Jagger, he may yet prove to possess that invaluable chameleon quality which enables these light-footed ones to escape from any trap. (The only admirable thing about them.)

I cannot close this particular pigeonhole without including, in a general sense, all musicians who have ever taken their shirts off onstage (usually prior to an ineffably tedious drum solo), all musicians who wear sunglasses onstage, and the bands of the early seventies techno-flash/Heavy Metal orbit, specifically Emerson, Lake and Palmer and Uriah Heep. I still cherish the remembrance of Uriah Heep's lead guitarist struggling about an Akron, Ohio, stage in what can only be described as pirate costume, complete with vast and unwieldy Captain Blood-style thigh-boots. Boots? They were more like angler's waders, and their broad, dashing tops continually caught in the poor sap's guitar lead.

Since those times, clothing has become simultaneously more colourful and exotic, and at the same time more self-deprecating, with the result that a modern artiste who finds him- or herself accused of sartorial disaster can always claim – and stand a chance of being believed – that the effect was *meant* as a joke. Pity.

The second category we touched upon was physical oddness. We decided that the Blue Öyster Cult qualified on account of their dwarved stature; to this list we might add the names of Barry White and Demis Roussos (grossly fat – Roussos used to be known widely as 'the singing tent'); Patti Smith (thin, pale, hairy legs and an incipient moustache) and the Bee Gees (ogreish teeth).

A third category – once epitomized by Bill Haley, not to mention each and every one of his Comets – comprises those whose absurdity lies in the fact that they are obviously, grievously too old. For general purposes you can take it that everybody over eighteen qualifies for membership, but in a particular sense one or two names stand out. The one name I feel quite unable *not* to mention is that of the British group the Stranglers. This group, like so many, appeared during the two or so years of the mid-seventies New Wave, and somehow succeeded, for a while, in being accepted as spokestwerps for one segment of British Yoof. After the fashion of the time they bellowed hoarse lyrics about the usual issues, with some unfashionable machismo titles thrown in for good measure, but afterwards veered off on their own thing. In many ways they are a reincarnation of the Doors.

They are also much too old and always have been. Whatever their other failings – and these are plenty – it's the lines on the Stranglers' faces and the receding hairlines on the Stranglers' pates, and the rasp and wheeze in the Stranglers' voices, which make them ridiculous.

Sometimes ridiculousness is momentary, a passing gleam from a malignant star; a glimpse caught out of context which remains with the delighted connoisseur of rock absurdity for the remainder of his days. Here is an example involving the Rolling Stones – perhaps the epitome of credibility in the rock world. Hoary, hairy, decadent, raunchy . . . I'd have to work pretty hard to make even the smallest dent in their credibility.

The Rolling Stones are, of course, usually known to their admirers simply as the Stones. It's a good, taut abbreviation, with connotations of solidity and permanence as well as marijuana. Now absorb this small but delicious tidbit: in Italy and Spain, where different tongues are spoken and adjectives normally *follow* nouns, the British rhythm and blues group are known, and advertised, as *i Rolling*. The Rolling! ('Say, coming to see The Rolling Saturday nite?' – 'The rolling of what, Cyril?') Now: take out a picture – any picture – of the group, sullen pouts, broken teeth, cocaine noses and all. Poise the photo on your mantelpiece. Absorb the facial expressions and let your mind drift gently over all they mean to you and The World. Now say to yourself, 'That, my friend, is a photo of a group called The Rolling!'

Observe the accrued credibility detach itself from the picture and flee, howling, up the chimney. Laugh yourself sick. Generally have a good time.

The very first episode of Tony Benyon's 'Lone Groover' cartoon strip, directly stimulated into existence by the Gaucho incident.

THREE
DON'T TRUST ANYONE UNDER THIRTY
infant politics

On 16 August 1969, at about 3.30 p.m., an amiable, bespectacled guitar-carrying person called John Sebastian appeared on the corner of a temporary stage on a farm in New York State, and addressed a several hundred thousand-strong crowd thus:

Uh wow man I mean like wow you know? I mean . . . like . . . wow, I mean man there's like man uh a quarter of a *million* of you out there I mean man a quarter of a million I mean like wow man like this is really . . . man, like I mean this is really something you know? (etc.)

I have heard some speeches from the rock and roll concert stage in my time but this will always be my personal favourite. There is perfection here, of a sort. For me, it sums up an entire generation – that to which, God help me and all of us, I belong.

The first thing to make clear is that in one respect Sebastian (former leader of the Lovin' Spoonful) was actually right. The best estimates all maintain that there really were more than 200,000 American hippies in one place at one time – that place being of course Woodstock, NY – and therefore, that that shambling, embarrassing, sentimental babble really did boom out by means of a colossal PA system over 200,000 plus close-packed heads. It is now clear that the reason the whole place did not explode with uneasy laughter at Sebastian's oratory is that *every one of those present was already talking* – to friends and other hippies in the toilet queues – *in precisely the same argot!* This incredible mishmash of non-words and redundant conjunctions therefore represented to the audience pretty much their own view of the Woodstock phenomenon.

I mean like wow. You know? Let's be honest, an argot that cannot stand being written down verbatim must immediately be suspected of being an unsatisfactory vehicle for ideas – or perhaps it is the ideas the argot was coined to express which are themselves deficient in coherence?

But Sebastian's little foray into the world of rhetoric was merely the beginning of the Woodstock experience. Over the next five or so days virtually every rock and roll luminary within five thousand miles of New York turned up and did a short set. Film cameras whirred, sound recordists recorded, and planeloads of pressmen, broadcasters and sightseers circled overhead, swearing incredulously.

As quite a few people who uttered them at the time would now prefer to leave forgotten, a great many hilariously inaccurate prognostications were put forth at the time as an immediate result of Woodstock. Here was the working of the Alternative Society! Had there not been less crime (no murder, anyway) at Woodstock than in any American city of 250,000 people over the same period of days? Had not 'quite a lot' of the garbage been picked up afterwards? Unscrupulous US politicians – mainly Democrats, I seem to remember – hastened to appear on TV saying 'Wow' and 'Like, I mean, uh . . .', having meanwhile combed their hair loose for once and left their neckties at home. People said: 'Maybe these kids have got something at that,' and for a while, despite the occasional cavilling voice from offstage, such was the general climate of opinion. Even Europe was amazed by Woodstock – the scale of it was impressive, after all – and immediately promoters of various levels of experience began planning other, similar events right across the Western world.

Within two months or so the second of these had taken place, at Altamont, a speedway track in California. Having passed up on Woodstock, I displayed a certain sense of occasion and actually went to Altamont. This time the general galaxy of attractions was rather less scintillating, but in the minds of the hundred thousand or so Californian punters this was no loss because the Rolling Stones were going to be there! Yes, Mick Jagger and his hardbitten team of slimy limeys were actually going to perform their hits 'Jumpin' Jack Flash' and 'Let's Spend The Night Together'! Among many others! Well, the Woodstock fantasy took a serious dent at Altamont. A young black man was murdered by Hell's Angels right in front of the stage, while the Stones – who had hired the Angels – huddled together for protection and cast appealing looks at their offstage minders, and Jagger, more daring than most, bleated 'Cool it, willya' into the microphone. Not a lot of the garbage was picked up by the departing Woodstock generation this time. The California cops waded in and busted left and right. There was a traffic jam ten miles long.

Neither this nor the well-known decline – into heroin, mugging, and pimping – of nearby San Francisco's Haight-Ashbury district, once World Hippyopolis, prevented a number of the more famous performers from writing (and performing) songs on the Woodstock theme. A film of the event was announced – not, as one briefly hoped, a spoof feature starring Woody Allen as John Sebastian, but a two-part instalment-plan flick, with all the big-selling names kept in and most of the turkeys winnowed out (but not for disposal; the turkeys appear in *Woodstock 2*).

Woodstock. Woodstock generation! Woodstock *nation*! Here's looking at a *Woodstock World*!

Woodstock, which had apparently – if only temporarily – appeared to confirm the higher sentiments so ably put by John Sebastian, was immediately followed by Altamont, which refuted them. But again the myth had taken charge. People were openly – had in many cases long been – devoted to the vague coalescence of ideas, some philosophical, some political or social, which had reached a (short-lived) apogee in the fields of Woodstock, NY. They were committed. That is the key word here. The best definition of 'committed' runs as 'being in a state of mind where some things seem more important than the truth'. So it proved. Woodstock gave the Alternative Society its moment of triumph, and was absorbed into (if I may so describe it) the corporate myth of the Now Generation, who wanted peace to be given a chance and who counted to three before asking, rhetorically, what they were fighting for. (The 'they' in this instance standing for the American nation and not the Woodstock nation.)

But if Woodstock was a brief moment of incandescent *cultural* triumph, the greatest achievement of the nation-within-a-nation was yet to come. For away in Indo-China, what the North Vietnamese army could never have done unaided, the Now Generation of Americans now did for them. The American government decided, in a series of increasingly hurried stages – especially towards the end – that the domestic unrest provoked by the Vietnam War was in the long term a greater threat to national stability than the loss in overseas American prestige. They pulled American troops out of that unhappy country South Vietnam – which of course then fell to the North Vietnamese – and in doing so sustained a geopolitical disaster which has permanently (*permanently* is the only possible word here) scuppered the United States' position in the world. Like a punch-drunk boxer, America has staggered from humiliation to wretched humiliation. Would Reagan conceivably have been elected if it weren't for the performance of Carter? Would Carter – who encapsulates the entire Iran disaster in his own self – have secured the trust of the American people had it not been for Gerald Ford before him, who, though obviously your sincere type of schlemiel, was a schlemiel none the less and moreover Nixon's nominee? As for Nixon . . . to many Americans, the man is a national humiliation in himself. How did he come to be elected? Because he *promised to end the war* – Lyndon Johnson's war in Vietnam – *with honour!*

As a matter of fact, America ended the war with maximum dishonour, but by the early seventies the anti-war movement (not all of whom, to be fair, were members of the Woodstock nation) was on top politically and would brook no further delay, and even Nixon was left with little room to manoeuvre. There then followed, in no particular order: (1) the overrunning of the entire peninsula as far as Thailand by fanatical communist troops and militias; (2) the persecution (punishment) of the South Vietnamese, and the subsequent, continuing tragedy of the Boat People; (3) the hideous atrocities of Pol Pot and the Khmer Rouge in Cambodia-Kampuchea; (4) the Chinese invasion of North Vietnam; and (5) the continuing wars and persecutions throughout former French Indo-China, actively stirred up by the Soviet Union (who backs Vietnam and now has a presence in that country equivalent to the early sixties American one), and China (who for some insane reason backs the heirs of Pol Pot).

Probably more Indo-Chinese have died since the American pullout than *before* it.

Since we have traced a causal chain right back from the deathpits of Cambodia as far as the flowerings of a successful domestic American anti-war movement, it must surely be legitimate to ask: were the anti-war protesters right?

It may be that they were, of course, and that the agitation which led to the American withdrawal produced the lesser of two evils. But is this true? It *seemed*, at the time, as if withdrawal would be the lesser evil from the point of view of the United States. But has it so proved? And what about the millions of helpless Asian peasants for whom it can be claimed that they would not have died had the Americans not pulled out? I don't pretend to know the answers myself, but it would be nice, wouldn't it, to hear from one of the famous quarter million who were at Woodstock, who sang 'One-two-three-what-are-we-fighting-for?' with such self-assurance, who applauded themselves with such self-satisfaction, who – in short – were so open, so free, so clear-eyed, so *committed*?

Nary a cheep so far.

Oh well, we've all been wrong on occasion, if not so royally as this. Even in the best of all possible worlds it would require a bit more water under the bridge before one could realistically expect 250,000 people to spring to their feet – wherever in the world they may be dispersed – and bawl 'We was wrong!' I concede (since we do not live in the best of all possible worlds) that it may never happen. And since the Vietnam War is now 'over' there would be little point in raking these dead ashes were it not for the fact that *the bastards are coming back for another go!* This time the Woodstock nation – we now see it never really went away – is making a second appearance in the geo-political arena. The subject? Nukes, both military and civil. And war generally.

It's a bit like roulette. The odds have no memory, so because (in my opinion) the Alternative Society got their basic calculation horribly wrong last time, it doesn't mean they're wrong *this* time. Does it? Myself, I prefer to ignore theoretical possibilities and study the form. And the formbook tells me that the last time a crowd of people apparently unable to tell the difference between the world as it is and the world as it is in pop-song lyrics took a hold on international affairs, the destiny prospects of mankind were significantly altered for the worse.

It is, of course, more than legitimate for (yawn) young people to take an interest in the world about them. There is much to see and do. Sex is available to many. Trains and planes exist merely to be ridden in. There are exciting foodstuffs to sample, energetic sports to enjoy. Sleep is fun. Films, too, can help a lot in broadening one's horizons.

Why, then, do so many of them take an interest in politics, which by common assent is the dreariest and most depressing of all human activities, made only worse for all concerned by the enthusiastic par-ticipation of clear-eyed amateurs. History is a dangerous guide to the future; but it is even more dangerous to ignore its lessons entirely – as 'young people' (and in case any doubt remains, I use this term as a synonym for 'immature people') are only too prone to do, not having read any. It is today well known (*sic*) that history is a bunch of lies and distortions, concocted by evil old men in order to cloud the clear light of truth and perpetuate evil political systems. Therefore it is incumbent on young people not to touch the stuff with a bargepole.

It's a point of view. I myself have read a bit of history (there is an abundance of cheap laughs if you know where to look), and from what I can remember there is no single recorded instance where the laying-down of arms by the clear-eyed has led to anything other than the immediate massacre either of the clear-eyed themselves or those for whose welfare they have been pleading. It is surely beyond doubt that the refusal of the European democracies to re-arm during the thirties was a direct cause of the Second World War, with its millions of dead. But (you say) the clear-eyed of the thirties, pacifistic idealists though they were, took up arms the moment war started (most of them, anyway) and did their bit. Perfectly true. But – sidestepping for a moment into What-might-have-been country – mightn't there have been *no* Second World War at all if the disarmers and idealists had simply kept their collective trap shut in the first place? Again, here we have an arguable case (at the very least).

One would have thought this awesome example might have deterred the Woodstock generation from their Vietnam position; that even today it might deter CND, whom I privately prefer to call the Orange Party,* from their daily-more-successful anti-nuke position. But, as we pointed out, to this miserable crew of philosophical hookers there is no such thing as a 'lesson of history'. They don't know or care that fifty years of continual, disgusting appeasement did not, in the end, save the Eastern Roman Empire from the ravages of the Huns; that a favourite ploy of the ancient Assyrians when besieging a city was to persuade the citizens therein to open their gates of their own free will, whereupon the Assyrians would butcher the lot; that, whatever the position of the weak may be in the next world, in this one they invariably go to the wall.

The alliance of 'rock culture' with the idealist strain in (Western) politics begins with the arrival of the Protest Singer and his vehicle for self-expression, the Protest Song.

In 1964 Barry McGuire had a worldwide hit with a famous first of this depressing genre, 'Eve of Destruction'.

'Don't you know/We're on the Eve of Destruction,' warbled Barry rhetorically, and he had something of a point, since the Cuban missile crisis was only just behind us. The 'destruction' we were on the eve of was, of course, nuclear war, and this idea was, in the early sixties, by no means implausible. So damned good an idea was it, in fact, that virtually within seconds (as it seemed), a whole trainload of Apocalyptists were attempting to follow Barry's END OF THE WORLD IS NIGH sandwichboard along the world's high street and, so they hoped, into the Top Twenty.

'A hard rain's gonna fall,' groaned Robert Zimmermann, a.k.a. Bob Dylan, and he too had considerable success with his records. In fact, within months, if not weeks, Bob Dylan had become accepted as the very model of a modern moaning minnie. He was the Protest Singer *par excellence*: the unkempt, attractively frizzy hair; the faded jeans; the badly tuned guitar slung around the neck; the curious contraption designed to hold a harmonica in place adjacent to the mouth; and, worst of all, the extremely silly corduroy cap perched on said frizzy locks.

The trouble, however, with being a modern-day equivalent of the Seventh Day Adventists (the jokers with the END OF THE WORLD sandwichboards) is that when the world *doesn't* end as predicted, the

*Orange Party: half-red, half-yellow.

doom merchant, if he or she is not careful and fast on his or her feet, tends to look a bit of a prat. I mean, imagine if Noah had gone to all that trouble, built his ark, loaded it with livestock and so on . . . and then what had followed had been nothing more than a few light showers, ideal for the spring crops? One must surely admit his credibility would have been strained. And, following from this, Barry McGuire's prediction ('eve' means 'eve' in my book) was wrong! Twenty years have passed and no destruction of the promised type has taken place. This may explain McGuire's tactful disappearance from human ken.

Bob Dylan solved the problem by retreating into obscure metaphor and 'poetry' – defined in his case as 'pleasing assonances devoid of meaning'. This (plus the ditching of both harmonica-holder and affected corduroy cap) did the trick! He translated himself into another metier entirely – the metier of rock and roll. Now this is a period I remember very well. I was there. That is, I was at the Royal Albert Hall, London, when Dylan played the second gig of his 1966 European tour – the first tour he had done with his new rock and roll format. I remember the reception he received. Thousands of cap-wearing, frizzy-haired former idolators absolutely *bayed* and *hissed* at the poor bastard as he staggered around the prestigious boards of the Albert. Why? Because he'd *gone electric*! He'd compromised with lowbrow pop culture and bought himself a backing band (actually a pretty good one by the standards of the day). Personally, I thought the whole Dylan enterprise much improved by the addition of some musicians of professional standard – but then, I wasn't there as a punter, but as the representative of a London music store which had rented a considerable quantity of expensive electric equipment to the Dylan entourage.

Being thus accredited, I was allowed backstage before the show. Being backstage, I actually found myself *in the same room* (gasp!) as Bob Dylan. Being in the same room as Bob Dylan (his friends called him Bobby, by the way), I was thus in an ideal position to see what a slob he was.

Bobby was seated in a battered overstuffed armchair, his eyes rolling, his speech slurred, his gestures uncoordinated. Was he, as one might assume, drunk as a skunk? Intoxicated, yes. The actual substance remains a mystery. It might have been cannabis; then again, it might have been heroin. Or downers (barbiturates). It's not important – I myself have frequently been in a similar condition (though not from heroin or downers).

'Waaargggh!' croaked the former Protest Singer. This was translated by the hovering toadies as 'Ho there – bring me a cup of tea!' A cup of tea was brought. A pot of honey was also furnished; its lid unscrewed. Tea and honey jar were placed on the arm of the overstuffed armchair, and all present – about a dozen – watched with reverence/

curiosity/repugnance as the megastar seized the honey and tipped it so that a substantial stream of the stuff flowed thickly into the tea. Time passed. Honey continued to pour. The tea began to overflow. 'Grrrrunnnngghkk!' commented the Biggest Thing in the Rock World, his eyes rolling in his head. With a convulsive movement he dropped the honey. A moment later a flailing arm had swept the repulsive brew clean off the chair and straight on to the lap of an adoring female seated intimately next to Bobby. She sprang to her feet with a cry of distress and left the room, re-emerging into the known world nearly a decade afterwards as the hopeful pop singer Dana Gillespie.

OK, so we all have our bad moments. I myself once drank so much at a record company banquet that I vomited; unable to leave the table, I was forced to retain and swallow the noxious mouthful thus obtained rather than deposit it on the tablecloth under the gaze of my dining companions. But then, I'm not, nor have ever been, the Biggest Thing in the Rock World. Nor was I within minutes of going on stage at the Royal Albert Hall at a crisis in my career.

But although I referred to Dylan as a 'slob' a moment ago, this anecdote is not without its brighter side. For one thing, I acquired a notable I-was-there story which did my later career as a pop journalist a bit of good. For another, there was a deeper symbolic meaning in Dylan's obvious unhappiness and incoherence which tends to reinforce my view of the Protest era. By getting loaded immediately before a major concert Dylan was subsconsciously expressing a perfectly justified contempt for the cap-wearing audience impatiently waiting for the moment when they could start booing and shouting 'Traitor!' (Also, he was expressing terror, which is a sensible reaction.) By putting honey rather than refined sugar into his tea he was displaying a praiseworthy desire to take care of his physical self, and by knocking the lot over Dana Gillespie he was, or could have been, intuitively rejecting the tinsel and gloss of the world of rock and roll.

So much for Bob Dylan. His career has remained with him, despite a serious motorcycle accident and, even worse, his conversion to Christianity.* Nowadays, when he sings onstage, he naturally delivers a slice of his mid-sixties Protest repertoire – but there's a telltale glaze in his eyes when he does so, the same kind of glaze I saw in Bill Haley's eyes in 1974 when I watched him sing 'Rock Around the Clock' for what must have been the 98,000th time in his badly dressed career. This glaze needs defining: it is the look of infinite weariness of a performer who – by the immutable laws of performing – must, *must* come through with the old hits. They have long ceased to have any meaning, least of all for him, but immutable laws are immutable laws.

*And back again.

To glimpse the torment involved, imagine that when you were eleven you won a prize for an essay at school. Now try to imagine how you'd feel if twice a night for the rest of your life you were obliged to read that same essay aloud.

Yes, a terrible price to pay – but at least Dylan got off Protest songs, almost got out of rock and roll politics. How about his peers and contemporaries?

Chief of these has got to be the folk-singer Joan Baez, an absolute contemporary of Dylan's and – as we hear – a pal as well. For me, and many others, Baez epitomizes rent-a-cause: Black Emancipation; Vietnam; and now No Nukes. Not all of these causes are asinine or dubious. Only a fool or a fascist would deplore the material and constitutional improvement in the day-to-day position of American blacks which – inadequate as it still is – can be attributed, at least in part, to the activities of those who drew the attention of the mass of US citizenry to the absurd and evil discrimination taking place against blacks, especially in the Deep South. Pop songs of the Baez type undoubtedly played a part in this conscience-stirring procedure, and all credit to the singers thereof for that. What – in my book – later made the trilly Baez soprano a sound of abhorrence was the way she – and others – followed through the initial and justifiable victory by lending support to *many* extreme positions subsequently taken by black militants – during the era of so-called 'radical chic'. When Malcolm X uttered racist statements about white people equalled in their unfairness and venom only by the meanderings of the Ku Klux Klan's Grand Dragon; when Stokely Carmichael and H. Rap Brown and Eldridge Cleaver swore revenge on their fellow-Americans in the name of their ancestors, and did a bit of it too; when the (white) Weathermen (who took their name from a Dylan song) went on a mindless rampage of violence, Joan was right behind them – to such a grotesque and egotistical extent that she found herself brilliantly satirized by those admirable people behind *National Lampoon* magazine. On a special lampoon LP they provided a track on which an eerily accurate Baez impersonator sings 'Pull the triggers, niggers, we're with you all the way . . . right across the Bay' – the point of the tag line being that while the stirred-up blacks demolished Oakland, Ca, she and her well-heeled 'committed' kind were genteely egging them on from the safety of San Francisco. The song is reported to have hurt the gentle Joan deeply; I bloody well hope it did.

Now, after a shaky and low-profile seventies, Joan Baez has recovered all her former sublime righteousness. Her clear and musical voice, her characteristically jangly (but by no means unpleasant) guitar, now ring out against nukes as once they resonated in favour of the Viet Cong – or, more accurately, against the people who were against the Viet Cong which, alas, amounts to the same thing in this cruel, cruel world. We (that is, Joan and Co.) shall, apparently, overcome. Overcome what? Overcome self-righteousness and self-love? No fear of that.

In the meantime, if anybody asks you 'Where have all the flowers gone?' reply, 'Underground, pal, but given the breaks they'll be up again next year.'

Well, the war ended, but not before Nixon had made a truly heroic attempt to follow his baser, shaft-the-commies instincts and welsh on the one thing that got him elected. He, and Henry Kissinger, not to mention the United States Air Force – by now in a slough of super-cynical despond – bombed the shits out of the Parrot's Beak in Cambodia/Laos, just as Lyndon Baines Johnson had bombed the shits out of North Vietnam (unfortunately missing Jane Fonda, who was greasing around Uncle Ho at the time). There were riots across America. Four people – all students – were shot, by a panicky National Guard contingent, on the campus of Kent State University in Ohio. A few days before, Nixon had referred – quite accurately and succinctly – to student arsonists in Santa Barbara, Ca, as 'bums'. The four dead of Kent State were virtually the first *bona fide* martyrs the (predominantly white and middle-class) Woodstock generation had so far produced, and in joyous celebration of this semi-sacred fact Neil Young, the Canadian castrato sound-alike, wrote a rousing paean of self-pity which he and his colleagues in the Crosby, Stills, Nash and Young group then recorded.

> Tin soldiers and Nixon coming,

piped Neil,

> We're finally on our own.
> This summer I heard the drummin'
> Four dead in Ohio.

Actually on that day in Ohio over one hundred people died, some from natural causes and seven from self-inflicted injuries including drug overdoses. But the vision of Nixon plus the FBI and the Narcs and the CIA all coming to get the Woodstock generation and give them a good duffing-up was too good to pass over.

Then there was the 'People's Park' episode.

This priceless piece of hippie nonsense took place in Berkeley, Ca, at about the time I was resident in the district, so again I had something of a view of the incident. As I recall it (those interested can check, probably in *Rolling Stone*, which almost certainly will have published gargantuan articles on the subject), a municipal park of no great size

in the middle of Berkeley was subjected to a mass squat of the committed, most if not all of whom were skiving off lectures at the nearby
UCLA campus. 'People at Berkeley are very radical, very committed,'
a friend had warned me in Los Angeles on learning of my destination;
and by God he was right. Teams of yowling hippies poured into the
grungy little bit of greenery and camped. Cops with Neanderthal phy-
siognomy tried to evict them. There were riots up and down the little
town. The park was ruined. I visited it about a week after a late battle
– when the authorities had temporarily withdrawn in disorder. A few
sullen scruffs were squatting in fairy rings amid *absolute devastation*.
It looked like Passchendaele after a wet weekend and a thirty-hour
bombardment from the Hun. Litter . . . cans . . . all kinds of revolting
crap littered the ground. PEOPLE'S PARK it said on the gate, and some
fey creatures had woven lots of flowers into the woodwork of the sign
commemorating the great victory. Not a flower growing in the park,
mind you – not one. They'd all been pulverized in the Cops *v.* Committed combats.

It was at about this time that one saw the *de facto* breaking-up of
the first phase of the Woodstock coalition. The naive twerps and
self-pity artists drifted away in one direction, gently deploring all the
violence 'on both sides', and stuffing cocaine up their noses like there
was no tomorrow. The committed were left behind in possession of
the field, a rump of activism. These were the people who'd gone on
'trashing' binges in Santa Barbara, Watts, Oakland, and Kent State.
They now began to call themselves by strange names. Weathermen,
Yippies, White Panthers . . . they were all more or less on the same
axis, though the Weathermen and other nutters like the Symbionese
Liberation Army (I ask you!) were the most violent. 'Violence is
groovy,' said Miss Bernadine Doorhn, one of the Weather People.
The Yippies alone retained some style. That is, they too 'trashed' (i.e.
destroyed) things mindlessly, but they were more roguish than your
normal hippie and consequently – to me, at least – more likeable.
Their leading lights soon boiled down to two: Abbie Hoffman and
Jerry Rubin. It was the latter who said, in a famous example of the
kind of one-liner that comes back to haunt you, 'Don't trust anyone
over thirty!' The White Panthers, the only one of whom became infamous was the twit John Sinclair, were a sort of combination of the
two, though they were in temperament closer to the Yippies than the
Weathermen.

The Yippies' finest hour was the wrecking of the Democratic Convention in Chicago, 1968 – thus ensuring the subsequent victory of the
Republican candidate, the archfoe Richard Nixon. For this several of
them, including Hoffman, stood trial. They were enabled to emerge
from this experience morally unscathed by virtue of the fact that the

presiding judge was a creature of such monumental authoritarianism that even Genghis Khan would have attracted public sympathy had he been in the dock loaded with photogenic chains.

They also organized an event wherein several thousand people attempted to link arms around the Pentagon and cause it to fly away. By now they were a low-farce movement at best.

The White Panthers' leader, John Sinclair, was busted for possessing a tiny amount of dope and received a savage and disproportionate sentence, again from a hanging judge modelled on Roy Bean. Once more one saw the authorities handling the whole Yippie thing in a paranoid fashion. The names of Sinclair and the black revolutionary Angela Davis were commonly linked at that time, though I can't quite remember why.

In general it became plain that the thing had run its course. At Woodstock, the original gonzo vision gave one last stoned belch of self-satisfaction and fell sideways onto a sort of giant transcendental tapestry cushion, reeking of patchouli and spangled with tiny mirrors. In desolate places across America, and occasionally in Europe, woe-begotten camps of dogged tribalists remained (he who has not seen a rain-soaked encampment of wigwams on a Welsh mountainside in winter has not lived). Terrorists were bumped off, or retired and went into conventional politics, or were caught, or fled abroad to dwell disconsolately in places like Algeria, living on falafel, failing to learn Algerian French, and denied both booze and smoking requisites by the fierce-eyed True Believers. Instead they were given Marx and Lenin and Mao Tse-Tung to read, with occasional light relief by way of Franz Fanon and that Bolivian man whose name I can never remember. (The ones breaking rocks at home were fortunate by comparison.) Some opened shops, a lot 'dropped in' again, subsequently carving business or teaching careers for themselves in the best tradition. (For some reason, many became attorneys-at-law.)

Pop stars swore off Protest and sang self-consciously upbeat songs with the words 'rock and roll' somewhere in the title. Those who made most money during this time kept quiet on politics thereafter, being in many cases grown suddenly so conservative that their own earlier essays into Protest theming must now have embarrassed them severely. But others, less successful, remained proportionately more committed. And there now appeared, in England, a subtle redefining of the next mode of popular youth politics no less influential than the supposedly traumatic effects of the 'British invasion' of the early sixties. It was in Britain that a (proportionately quite large) activist rump found for itself a whole new ballgame – or rather, an old ballgame with a new angle.

I refer to the 'Rock Against' syndrome.

The tacit implication behind this British phenomenon was that Rock (the 'rock' of the common praenomen) was itself an entity of political stature, equivalent to a Sixth or Seventh Estate, on a par with the House of Lords or the established Church or the older professions both in its unshakable homogeneity and its right to be taken seriously. Therefore 'Rock' meant 'We of the Rock World'. What, precisely (some of us asked, timidly) was this world of Rock that so demanded – by the fearless candour of its chosen name slogan – to be heard? How was it structured? What of its hierarchy? Whose voices sang the loudest, and were they entitled to so disproportionate a hearing? Was it not in fact a reappearance of the Woodstock world? Yes, but with a new determination and resolve. 'No more pussyfooting around with weedy non-titles like "The Alternative Culture" and "Radical Opinion," it seemed to say. So this useful word 'rock', which until now had meant a bodily action, i.e. the rocking to and fro of a person performing the appropriate dance steps, now acquired a shift of connotation, and became stony, permanent, diamond-hard, immovable. Rock of Gibraltar! Rock Hudson! Rock and roll itself – the music – became 'rock music' as part of the same transformation. As if to leave one in no doubt of the intention, the second word of the common praenomen was AGAINST. Rock against what? Against anything you like, it seemed.

The first thing Rock was against was RACISM. Like a knightly warrior of old hoping to make his name in the lists, Rock strode out of the ranks of the army of the righteous, named his opponent, excoriated him, and challenged him to single combat.

It was a soul-stirring experience, I don't think.

The opponent turned out to be not so much racism in its wholesale, subsurface and therefore hardest to bring to battle sense, but Racism Incarnate in the form of a small axis (sic) of political parties of the extreme (patriotic) Right in Britain, centred around the National Front. Rock Against Racism now found itself automatically part of a wider political front called the Anti-Nazi League. The engine of this operation was the Socialist Workers' Party. How much they thought they were battling the negative attitudes of the thirties and how much they were set upon recreating them must remain a matter of opinion. It turned out that various members of the board (so to speak) of Rock Against Racism were also members of the SWP, whose finest hour this was to prove. The Anti-Nazi League was created specifically to confront the National Front, at first in propaganda and in attempting to see that existing laws against offensive literature were properly enforced, later (but not much later) in what we now have to call 'direct action', i.e. by confronting the National Front physically in carefully staged counter-demonstrations. The police were in the middle, but in the minds of the racial minorities in whose boroughs these clashes usually took place, and certainly in the minds – and propaganda – of the Anti-Nazi League and the SWP newspaper *Socialist Worker*, they were seen as being on the side of the National Front marchers. As many policemen were (and are) undeniably racist in their approach to their job, this was not without foundation. But on demo days the police could not be seen to be favouring one side. This problem was solved when the Anti-Nazi League attacked the National Front marchers, and the police as well. In the resulting melee the Front appeared as innocent bystanders alongside the ferocious, and on one occasion fatal, battles between police and counter-demonstrators. In the end the problem went away when the authorities took the shortest way out and began to ban National Front marches. In other words, the promise of continuing extreme mob violence every time a political organization exercised its (admittedly provocative) right to march reinforced the (hitherto reluctant) practice of banning political demonstrating *because of what the demonstrators' opponents might do!*

So the campaign of the Anti-Nazi League – which included Rock Against Racism – succeeded, not in destroying racism itself, but in limiting the political rights of their direct opponents and in so doing of course surrendering their own. And mine, too, which is what matters to me. I don't know about you.

A resounding rebuff thus administered to racism and Nazis in England, the Rock Against movement therefore assumed, with relief, its overtly Marxist form. Race remained an issue, now with the police cast as the prime target for opprobrium (again, not without considerable justification). But other, more traditionally socialist, aims were (effortlessly) grafted onto the existing structure. Whole new and interesting categories of underprivileged were discovered. Minorities gave birth to mini-minorities. Aquarius' not-so-sanguine cousin Agitprop took the reins of the age. The synonymity of the Spirit of Rock and the political Left became taken for granted in the most airy way possible. Political protest became more localized and therefore specialized, with certain large-scale internationalist issues being sure of respectful coverage.

Thus, from the idea that to protest against specific events or policies (i.e. Vietnam) was the right and duty of every citizen, we have moved to the implicit idea that to be in a *state of constant protest and rebellion* was, and is, the only (and undisputed) role for the enlightened person to play. The idea of – forgive me – ongoing injustice being permanently built in to the relationship between rulers and ruled has been planted; as any Leninist or especially Trotskyist will tell you, an essential foundation for a revolutionary society. Make one if you can't find one.

The history of rock and roll politics in the seventies, therefore – in the UK at least – is of gross and facile manipulation by the political left.

Did this make life in Britain any happier?

A big No.

Gone were the dear, dead days of the Edgar Broughton Band bellowing 'Out Demons Out!' from the back of a lorry in Paddington. Of the sincerely Maoist group Henry Cow, whose trick and habit it had been to waste incredulous writers' time with boring monologues about collectivism. Now virtually every post-teen numbskull with a silly name and designed-to-shock outerwear wanted to sound off, and why not? If there really *was* some mysterious entity, some preternatural manifestation of gestalt, called Rock, then surely these, its princes and princesses, were its natural spokespeople? With the easy polish which distinguishes all true elites, they assumed the verbal leadership, the philosophical mantle, of the angry young – now beginning to be referred to, ominously for them, I thought, as 'the masses'.

Heaven had an answer. Heaven always does. Elvis died. Barely had the King been planted in the ground when the great Clean-up Campaigner in the Firmament, cackling wildly, let go with the second barrel.

Down from the tree fell John Lennon.

And from the West came a great silver bird flying, and from the bird came a great voice, saying, lo, art thou ready down there for cruise missiles?

FOUR

NOT ONLY CARTHARTIC
BUT SEMINAL
the music press

It is sometimes said that the music business is corrupt. And so it is.

But is the music *press* corrupt? It depends on what you mean by corruption.

First of all, I know of no instance where a writer has been offered cash money to review an act favourably – or indeed at all. This does not mean it has never happened (it almost certainly has); it is just that music writers are normally handled in a different way.

This is the sort of thing I mean:

MANAGER or PR: Hi. Wondered if you'd like to review the boys' next gig.

REPORTER: Actually, I'm rather –

MANAGER or PR: In Hawaii.

REPORTER: – at a loose end. I'd be delighted to come.

And indeed he will be! He'll be flown to Hawaii, met at the airport by a limousine and whisked away to a moderately good hotel where PR people will offer him cocaine and fruit. He will eat Surf 'n' Turf and drink copiously and entertain hopes of getting laid and all he has to do by way of return for all this munificence is . . . simply allow himself to be driven in luxury to a nearby stadium, go backstage, partake of viands and more cocaine while wearing a special plastic badge that shows how important he is and . . . then write about. That's all.

Hard cases who can hold out against all this (i.e. either not accept the freebie, or go on the freebie and *then* stitch up the act afterwards) do exist, but there are precious few of them. I have never displayed a great deal of scruple. Like almost everybody else, I find myself accepting the freebie, then producing obligingly laudatory copy afterwards; it's hard to be ungracious to someone who's just flown you to Hawaii, all expenses paid. This is how the system works and if you care to call it corruption that's fine with me.

Right: 'Like a volcanic combination of coypu and Christmas tree . . . The Slade's 'Dancing Dave' Hill – and the picture that initiated a new train of thought

Below: The lowest point? Sid Vicious pictured posing at the Chelsea Hotel, New York, with the knife he used two days later to kill Nancy Spungen (right)

Above: The Benefits of Dying
at Home, Part One: This is
an off-day at Gracelands,
Memphis, Tennessee, where
Elvis lies a-mouldering. For 99
per cent of those who pass
humbly by to pay their
respects, this is by far the
closest they will ever have got
to 'the King'

Right: The Benefits of Dying at
Home, Part Two: 'Never croak
in Paris, France' should be
engraved on the consciousness
of all rock and roll stars
considering the state of the far-
flung corner of a foreign field
that is for ever Jim Morrison.
The fat French *flic* cops francs
for pointing out the graffiti he
is nominally supposed to
prevent

Left: The long-lost Jackie Dennis. When the author came to search the files for the original kilted portrait, it had disappeared – undoubtedly acquired by an anonymous fellow-connoisseur

Examples of involuntary ridiculousness: Bill Haley, 'grievously too old' in his declining years; and Patti Smith – the hairiest legs this side of Wolfman Jack

Above: 'A working telephone exchange in a medium-sized industrial town' – Keith Emerson with Moog synthesizer

Right: Rick Wakeman takes a bow complete with silver cloak. Note reverently applauding fellow-musicians

Facing page: How gauche can a gaucho get? The cigarette is held steadily enough, but doesn't that telltale glare in the eyes denote a premonition that all may not end as it should? Bryan Ferry bluffs it out anyway

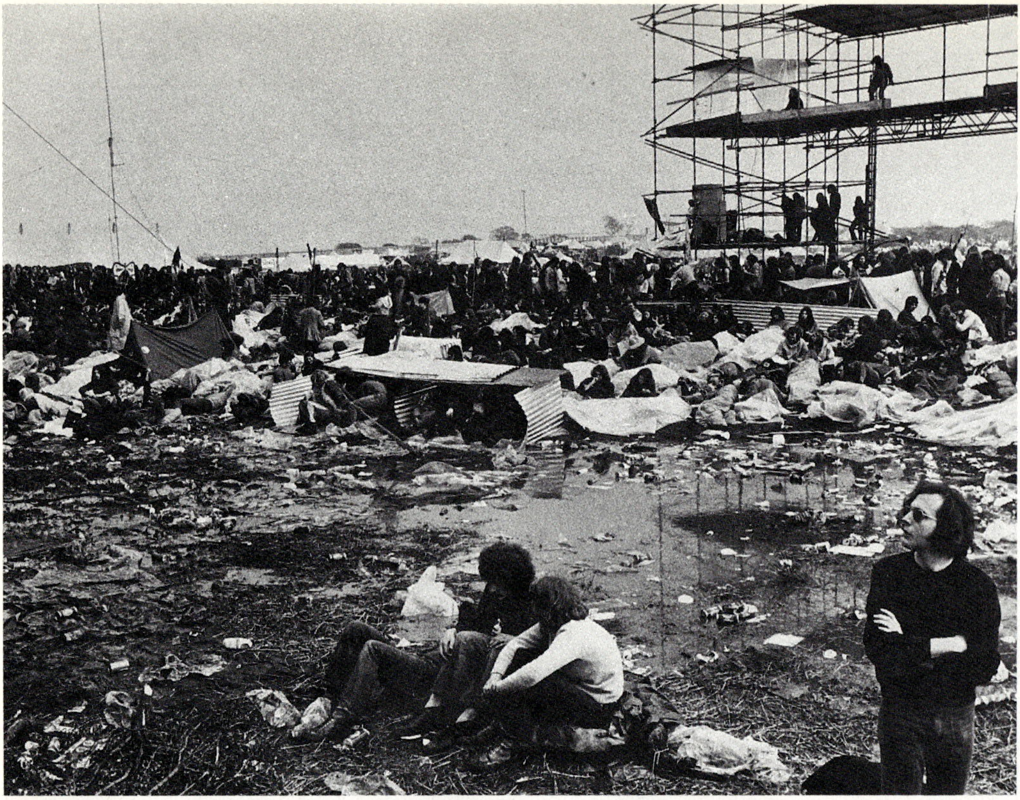

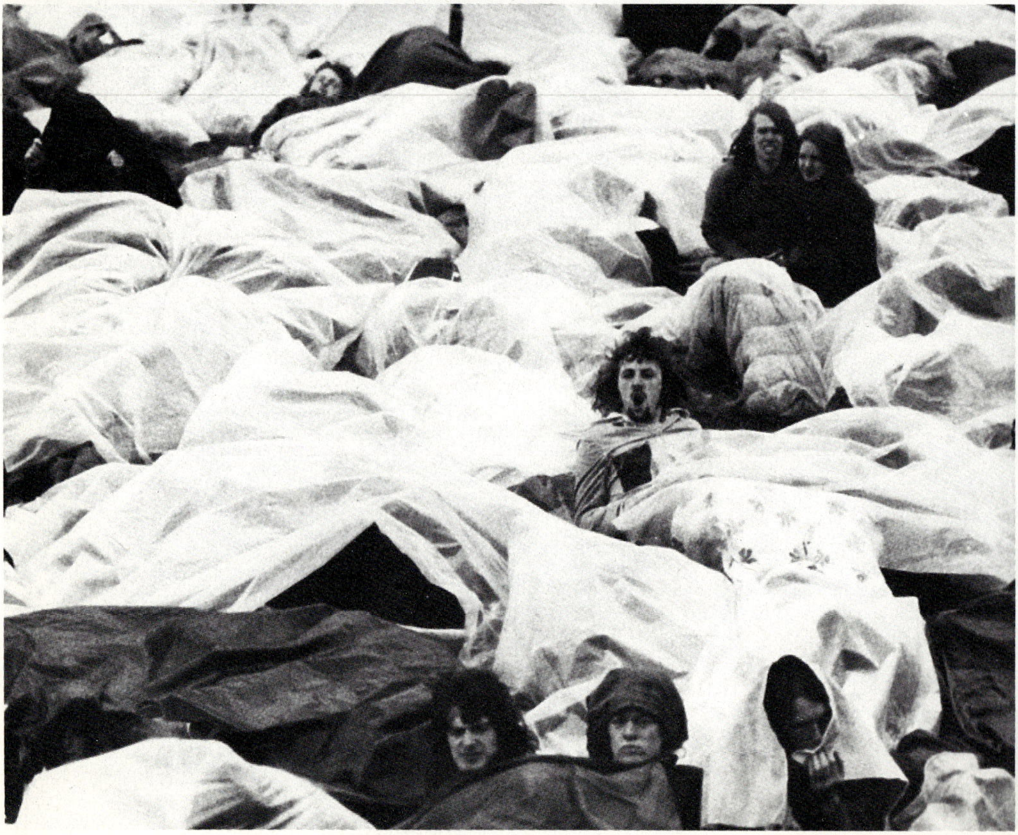

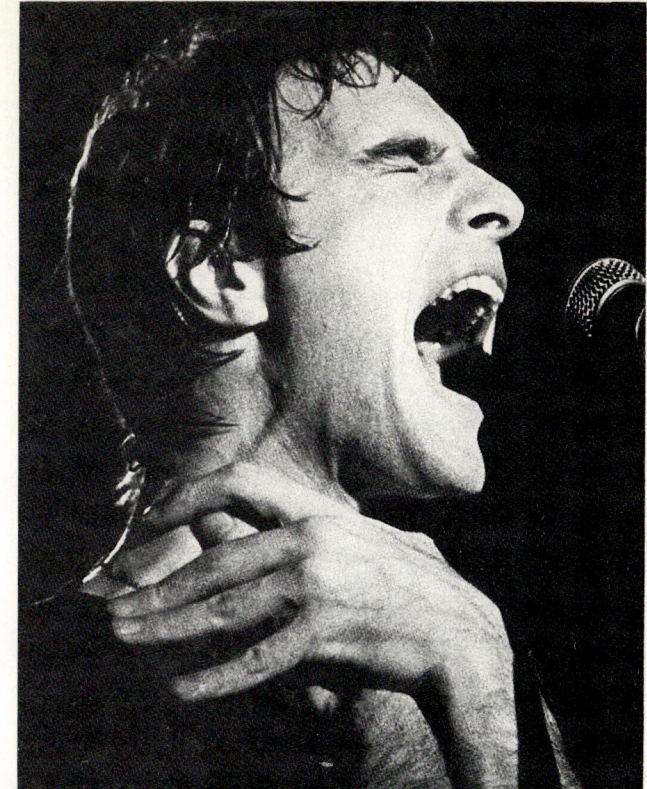

Facing page:
Festival Joy, Parts One and Two:
Above, Bickershaw, Lancashire,
started the 1972 season off well.
Below, Lincoln – 'all was misery on
a scale not seen since the Somme' –
finished it. NB: the punters in either
case are presumably those same
people who would object loudly if
chemical-warfare civil defence
rehearsals were to be staged

Right and below: Steve Harley
attempts self-strangulation after the
Crystal Palace fiasco; and Crystal
Palace, London

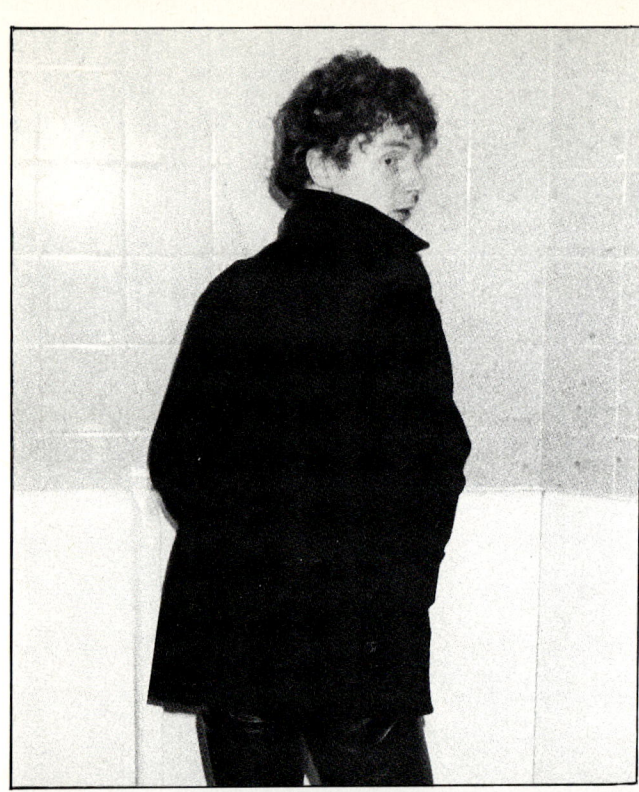

Left: One of the very few winners: Malcolm McLaren, impresario of punk rock, pictured having a quiet chat with a friend

Below: 'And faces contorted in ham-actor torment' – archetypal Guitar Cowboy of his age, Alvin Lee

The underlying problem is that music papers are not real newspapers any more than music journalists are real journalists. Real newspapers have travel budgets of their own to ensure editorial independence; real journalists would never dream of putting their objectivity at risk in such a way (in an ideal world anyway). But music journals are not newspapers, they are magazines. Magazines acknowledge no higher calling than making money for the proprietors and are more than willing for their editorial staff to go on foreign freebies (by-lines from abroad snazz up articles no end) *provided they are not called upon to pay*. So if the hack wants a spot of hedonism and star treatment, he has to rely on third parties like record or management companies. Trips are a perk, and the practice in these cases is to render unto the bestower of the perk whatsoever he desireth.

When the first purely pop periodicals first appeared, in the middle fifties, their power was, and was perceived to be, an extension of Tin Pan Alley's. There was no critical writing at all. Every record was either a Hit or a Miss. No other criteria were relevant. The journalists themselves were indistinguishable, physically or mentally or in any other way, from the PR people who handled the acts, and 'copy' and 'handouts' were virtually interchangeable.

Since that time – in the UK at least – the music papers (called 'the comics' by the music business generally) have become a mini-establishment in their own right. In the British magazine business virtually *all* publications are national. Therefore in Britain the pop press wields a great deal – some say a disproportionate amount – of power.

In what form do music journalists wield this power? One function they have always had is reviewing – either records or live performances.

The late fifties and early sixties were a golden age when even the editor of one of the largest-selling publications could take his duties so lightly that he apparently saw no point in going through the formality of actually listening to the discs he was officially appraising. Ninety-nine times out of a hundred (given the standards of the day) this procedure would have been fail-safe; on occasion it produced embarrassing failure. 'Duane', began one review – a 45 rpm single by the (exclusively instrumental) guitarist Duane Eddy – 'is in fine voice as usual.' By and large his attitude was typical of those easygoing times, and in case my reason for relating this story be misunderstood, *I wholeheartedly approve*.

Not all reviews, though, are of recorded product. Nowadays even more than ever before, music writers are expected to take a keen interest in the performing standards of the luminaries. This is a more difficult proposition altogether. If you think about it for a moment, a rock and roll concert – from the point of view of the hack who desperately wishes to be elsewhere – is a kind of prison. There you are, the honoured and sole representative of your journal, and about to go onstage any moment are the idiots you've been sent to review. How to get out of it? You eye the monster stacks of amplification equipment: they bode misery and evil. How to spare yourself the agony of sitting (or worse, standing), forcing your features to register happiness and approval, throughout a cacophonous and extremely boring public rendition of the act's latest *meisterwerk*? You could 'split' – but at the end of the day you still have x column inches to fill, with presumed hordes of readers scanning your prose in the honest hope that your opinions coincide with their own. Yes, it's a problem.

The remedy lies in 'reviewing from the bar', which is both a trade metaphor and a literal description of the music hack's alternative.

I should emphasize that this option is not for the green or the faint-hearted. You absolutely *have* to know the kind of thing to write, the kind of verbal camouflage to incorporate, in order to disguise the fact that you spent the entire concert in the bar upstairs while, down below (in a kind of Dante's *Inferno*-esque rerun), a sea of arm-waving, peace-sign-making, great-coat-wearing, head-banging dullards or Mohicans were disporting themselves frenziedly while bathed in about a million watts of aural garbage. This means you must be (a) familiar with the genre of act on display, and (b) able to assemble a reasonably accurate list of the numbers performed, together with any other important minor details like encores (number of) and effects (special or unintended), for the hard core of your subsequent review.

Tacit allies can be found from among the ranks of the PR fraternity, many of whom, after all, are in a similar fix to yourself. But there is a certain form to these sorts of negotiations, and conventions must be observed or self-respect will belatedly be invoked and a Frost Curtain of non-cooperation will descend.

Here is an example of how *not* to make such a phone call.

REPORTER: Hi. Look, just couldn't face it last night after all . . . all that total shit. Jeez! It was bad enough from the bar, which in case you didn't see me was where I was. Mind just reeling off the old running order? Got to write something, after all. Heh heh.

This comes under the heading 'Candid but tactless', and will surely ruffle all but the most cynical feathers. The next example is much more *à la mode*.

REPORTER: Hi. Yeah, I really dug the gig . . . that's right . . . no, I'm not surprised you didn't see me . . . down at the front, where I always am . . . I always feel you can't really review a gig unless you *get down* with the *people*, know what I mean? Right on! Look, reason I'm calling, in the crush to get away afterwards, musta dropped my running order. Mind giving it to me again one time, know what I mean? Brilliant! (etc., etc.)

However, on no account attempt this valuable and time-saving ploy with any of the dedicated and alert sort of PR, and especially not with manager-figures. For these latter types – or rather, for their 'boys' – no praise can ever be excessive, no criticism ever anything but malevolent and biased. Dealing with such creatures is a nightmare of tension – they watch you anxiously if you start in too heavily on the supplies of booze, and then snap some poor 'personal roadie's' head off if your glass is empty. You are conscious, while in their company, of their weighing you up in publicity-column-inch terms, comparing you on cost grounds with, say, a 10 × 4-inch spot colour ad. They are a deadly tribe, fully capable of telling your editor, by way of a 'casual' phone call, that no, they didn't actually see you at the gig and (on being pressed by the editor), yes, they did actually see you in the upstairs bar while the concert was at its climax, drunk as a skunk. They can cost you your job! No – the enterprising hack must steer clear of these sons-of-bitches altogether and do half an hour of real journalism, i.e. he must assemble the running order by way of some *Daily Planet*-style legwork.

A snippet here . . . a tidbit there . . . it all adds up, if he knows what he's doing and whom to ask. In his colleagues he has a field of exploitation ready to hand; but beware! this too can often turn out to be an elephant trap.

REPORTER 1: Morning. How did it go last night?
REPORTER 2: How did what go?
REPORTER 1: The Toadstools' gig at Wembley.
REPORTER 2: I didn't go.
REPORTER 1: (Seriously alarmed) *You didn't go?*
REPORTER 2: You heard. Anyway, I thought you were going.
REPORTER 1: Jesus Christ.
REPORTER 2: (Maliciously interested) You didn't go either? I thought you were down to review it?
REPORTER 1: (Hollowly) I am. I didn't go because I thought you were going. I was going to get the running order from you.
REPORTER 2: (Sententiously) Well, I didn't go.
REPORTER 1: Don't rub it in, you bastard.

But music writers have other duties besides reviewing.

Most full-time staffers, for example, cannot, try as they might, avoid doing the occasional interview. Magazine sales in this field utterly depend on an abundance of celebrity names that can be bannered on the front cover. Modish names. This requirement can to some extent be met by means of the last-minute, last-ditch, 'think piece' device (*The Early Work of BRUCE SPRINGSTEEN: a dissenting reappraisal* or *Seminal Influences #23: GRAND FUNK RAILROAD*). But this is cheating, and everybody knows it. At the end of the day you have to come back to the interview.

In the pop paper format an interview means the interrogation, by a staff writer, of a Prat of Renown, on the subjects of his music, his likes and dislikes, his political views, his lyrics (where these differ from his political views), his possessions, his last and next LPs, his forthcoming or ongoing nationwide tour, and other tripe of absolutely no value whatever. They are hell. Interviewing is a chore of the first magnitude, almost always uncomfortable, embarrassing, tedious and time-consuming, and very few writers derive any pleasure or benefit from it. Very few of them are any *good* at it, since successful interviewing requires the ability to shut up from time to time. (I was a mortal offender in this respect: embarrassment, nervousness, boredom – all these things invariably made me rabbit on like a ninny; and every time I played back the cassette tape, I found myself cringing with embarrassment at my own nonstop drone.)

If interviews are such hell for journalists, how do the interviewees feel about them?

I don't suppose any currently practising music writer will take issue with me if I say that almost all interviews are disliked, in some way, by the interviewed person. Their views are never fully represented. They are misquoted, they say (and indeed they very often are). The more self-important the interviewed artiste, the less likely he or she is to be satisfied with the written interview.

To complicate matters, in the last decade music writers have superficially abandoned hackdom and are now committed (definition of 'committed' can be found in the previous chapter). They also aspire. As a result, writing standards have suffered grievously, while simultaneously articles have grown longer and longer.

The following is an example of the kind of atrocity the current crop of music writers are capable of. (I've pulled some raw work myself in my time, and know others equally guilty, but this, I am ready to admit, is outside my class.)

Under the piston stroke of the mass media, of open and subliminal advertising, even our dreams have grown more uniform. Like our bread, much of our manner is becoming prepackaged. It is only in secret that we celebrate the insolent wonder of the ego, that we inhale – oh, riddle of sensuality – the smell of our own ordure.

Knowing begins with the awareness of the deceptiveness of our common sense perceptiveness, in the sense that our picture of physical reality does not correspond to what is 'really real' and, mainly, in the sense that most people are half-awake, half-dreaming and are unaware that most of what they hold to be true and self-evident is illusion produced by the suggestive influence of the social world in which they live. . . .

And a little later on in the same article:

He now had to experience himself . . . the body was surely not the SELF, nor more was the play of the senses, yet thinking was not it either, nor reason, nor acquired wisdom. . . .*

The main problem with the interview format – leaving aside the above – is that it rests on a fallacy: is there any good reason why a chap who is deft, say, on the guitar should reasonably be expected to be remotely interesting on any subject *other* than guitar (if on that)? To which the accepted counter is: aha, but by no means *all* pop chappies play the guitar. Many write songs, complete with controversial lyrics! Surely the purveyors of effective song lyrics qualify as poets or at least commentators and therefore deserve the chance to amplify and expand upon their triumphantly teenage thought processes?

The routine, boringly humdrum but unassailable riposte (i.e. if his lyrics are so effective, why does he feel the need to amplify them? And if they aren't effective, why is it proposed to interview him at all?) fails to take into account the innate desire to pronounce. To state, to ideologize, to lecture. To boldly go. To wishfully think. Once more than happy to reveal nothing more intimate than details of his domestic cuisine, a pop star now demands a platform.

Consider the case of the currently fashionable and successful Anglo-Irish pop group, Dexy's Midnight Runners. They appeared towards the end of the seventies, wear loose-fitting clothing *au paysan* and have since scored several Top-Twenty hits.

Dexy's Midnight Runners have something to say. So much do Dexy's have to say that in 1980, after two years' solid support from the music press and vastly increased gig fees to prove it, Dexy's bought advertising space in 'the comics' in order to announce, in the most ludicrously pompous terms imaginable, that as they (Dexy's) had been gravely dissatisfied so far with the lamentable failure of the music press to represent their views with sufficient exactitude, henceforth a *cordon sanitaire* would be drawn between Dexy's and the interview situation. Whenever Dexy's wanted to say something to the public, they would buy advertising space – as they had done in this instance – and use it to issue a statement.

*Publication: *New Musical Express*, 6 November 1982. Article: 'The Other Side of Silence' (actually an interview with attractive blond David Sylvian of Japan) by one Paul Morley. When I went to the *NME*'s offices in search of material of this sort, staffers queued up to thrust samples of this man's work at me for consideration. After reflection, I chose the above, but in all honesty I could have taken my pick . . . and not just from Morley's prose either.

Bizarre, I agree, but there is more to the story than a cautionary tale of runaway egos – it is also a sign that, in one aspect at least (the potential controversiality of interviews), music journalism has at last come to resemble real journalism. The relationship between the pop artiste and the music hack has for some years now been closely akin to the adversarial relationship which exists between politician and TV interviewer. Which, of course, implies that rock stars have come to resemble politicians.

What Dexy's Midnight Runners *did* assess correctly was that, in this matter of being interviewed – and feeling as committed as they did about any number of complicated issues – they were on a hiding to nothing. Not one of the Palaeolithic hacks with whom the band had dealt in the past was even remotely capable of doing justice to Dexy's Midnight Rhetoric. But – and this is where they went astray – where cannier heads might at least have mulled over the possibility of simply not being available for interview, Dexy's Midnight Rhubarb apparently never considered this excellent alternative. The idea of *not* pronouncing, of not talking at all, clearly failed to cross the collective mind.

Postscript: the group actually did take advertising space on two or three further occasions before nerve failed and/or wiser counsels prevailed.

A considerable amount of antipathy exists between the music press and those whose doings and sayings they report. Mostly this takes the form of the cold shoulder, the sneered aside, the hostile attitude, and the faithfully reported insult. And the artistes are just as bad! Of physical violence there is very little. Occasionally a road manager will shoulder a hack rudely aside, and hacks have been known to end up in rich artistes' swimming pools, along with the rich artistes' Bentleys. No hack, to my knowledge, has ever been shot. But hacks have been humiliated – and in return, they have hit back with their immeasurably more powerful weapon.

A lot of punters think that music papers pick on people, and so they do. I've done it myself, for no good reason at all other than blind malice. It happened several times; some aspect of an artiste – his hair, his voice, his face, his lyrics, any old thing – would strike me as not only ludicrous (the Dave Hill Effect) but downright offensive! Over a period of months, working quietly and with stealth, I would set out to needle the victim by means of headlines, references and unsigned witticisms in the gossip column. Naturally, the needled one soon began to suspect a hidden hand working his destruction (it never took him long to find out who it was), and pretty soon after that bitter judgements on my person would be reported back to me by my colleagues. Battle would be joined. Often as not, as soon as the needle match became generally apparent, a good many of my colleagues would joyously enter the fray. It was as if a long-pent-up reservoir of snide had been suddenly uncorked.

While it would be too much to claim that a new style of music journalism was initiated by one staffer's paranoid hate fantasies, it is certainly true that at about that time – the early seventies – music journalism suddenly found a use for good old-fashioned subjective invective. The polarization of the formerly cosy hack–ham relationship begins from this date.

Another thorn in the flesh of the music writer is the comprehensive body of libel laws which persists in making life difficult for the mean-minded – at least in the UK (these things are easier in the USA).

I in a subediting capacity once royally libelled a well-known British writer by calling him a 'hack' in a headline. As a matter of fact, I had taken this useful (but *prima facie* libellous) term from the copy and, at the time not knowing any better, set it in 36 point extra bold type. The libelled writer immediately sued the magazine, and the magazine had to pay him seven hundred quid; not a lot, but enough to cause estrangement between the then editor and myself. I thereby learned a useful lesson.

From the artiste's point of view suing a music paper for libel is a dodgy business – thank God. This does not mean to say that the threat is never used. On the contrary, it is. A particularly dicey moment arose one day when the editor was on holiday. It happened that in the issue before his departure one of our more flamboyant writers (in fact the same chap who had called the famous writer a 'hack' a few years before) had reviewed a new LP offering by the British singer/actor David Essex. In his review he had likened Essex's singing voice to that of a constipated stoat. Within hours of the issue hitting the stands, Essex's manager-figure was onto the editorial offices, raising hell. As I was in charge, I took the call.

It was a trying experience, not made any easier by the presence of the guilty party – plus other hacks, all in turbulent mood – in the editorial office at the time. Once I had established, with the Essex manager-figure, the precise wording of the phrase which had caused such offence (unwisely repeating this aloud and thereby causing the office to collapse into giggling uproar), I set about trying to save our asses from litigation. What the juvenile idiots around me didn't appear to realize was that I was fighting very hard to persuade the Essex manager-figure not to reach for his attorneys; and the only way open to me to achieve this was to employ all the casuistic filibustering techniques at my command.

This came down to arguing that the term 'constipated stoat' did not constitute a *prima facie* libel since there was no common or received opinion that a stoat, constipated or not, sang especially badly. 'For all you or I know,' I said firmly, 'the writer in question might well have meant it as a compliment!'

While I was saying this the writer in question was kneeling in front of me with a finger up each nostril, waggling his ears and squinting.

The Essex manager-figure eventually swallowed this garbage – or more likely simply became fed up with the conversation – and rang off. But it had been a close shave.

So far, as we have seen, music writing is a job with very mixed blessings.

You get a reasonable salary, and trips abroad (twenty-four hours of fat living sandwiched between two days of airplane terror, perhaps four times a year), but in return are automatically, tacitly, unquestioningly beholden to your hosts. You have to spend a large proportion of your time listening to records and going to gigs – your *own* time, that is; in the firm's time you write about them. You have to go repeatedly through the dreary business of the statutory interview, facing at best boredom and quite often outright hostility. The interview will be tedious and difficult to write, and whatever you write the subject won't like it. Before long you find yourself on bad terms with almost everybody you've ever written about. This produces tension, which can only be relieved by random spitefulness which – as we are told – endangers the very soul.

You will be subjected to real abuse several times a year and have an outside chance of being thumped by somebody. You will drink too much and probably get haemorrhoids. And to add to it all, the job doesn't really lead anywhere.

Occasionally even more sinister perils lurch, cackling, into sight.

Many years ago a friend of mine was working as a staff writer on a major British music weekly. The period was Middle Beatlemania, and my friend had just completed a purely routine, respectful, bland, uncontroversial interview with John Lennon. He gave in his copy to a subeditor and a day or so later went to the printers, together with several colleagues, to put his share of the paper to 'bed'.

'We were busy that day and I didn't get a chance to look round the other pages while they were still on the stone,' he remembers. 'Nor did I read the newly printed issue, as I usually did, on the train home. In fact, my wife got to it before I did.

'After about ten minutes I realized she was looking at me in a peculiar way. Then she said: "This John Lennon piece of yours. . . ."

'I grabbed the paper and read my article. I just couldn't believe my eyes. The subeditor had put my whole feature into what I can only call an interesting new light. For example, where I had originally written *John reaches for his cigarettes and lights one* the sub had altered this to *John reaches for a cigarette, his shiny black leather jeans taut across his slender buttocks* – or something very like that. These changes were all over the article.

'I eventually managed to convince my wife but I was never really able to approach the subeditor on the matter.'

I'LL CONDUCT THE STRINGS
HE CAN PLAY MOOG
YOU'RE ON SPOONS
the path of musical pretension

Elevations 9 began again, and this time continued. I devoted myself to the horrible task of listening to everything that was being played: the popping of the bongoes, the wailing of the sitar and the sticky thudding of the bass guitar as well as Roy's *obbligato* . . . a momentary increase in the nearby hubbub distracted my attention from the stage sufficiently to bring it home to me that the central aisle, in which earlier there had been about as much movement to and fro as in a village street on a fairly busy morning, was now more than half full of people shuffling unhurriedly but steadily in one direction: towards the door. . . . Some sort of climax evidently approached: the fiddle mounted to a high note and held it, Pigs Out did another series of as it were chords and sustained one that quite closely resembled that of the 6/4 on the dominant – the signal, in true classical style, that the accompanying forces are about to shut up while the soloist displays his technical skill in a cadenza. . . .

Without sparing me the trill on the supertonic that classically heralds the return of the accompaniment, Roy was briefly reunited with Pigs Out and brought his composition to a close in something like silence. . . . *Elevations 9* had been a complete flop. I had devoutly hoped it would be, and yet I found myself overwhelmed with feelings of anticlimax and defeat.

Bolsover lit a cigarette. 'Was it any good from your point of view?'

'No. It was . . . No. Was it any good from yours?'

'No.'

(From *Girl, 20* by Kingsley Amis)

At the very beginning of rock and roll, it was quite unnecessary to be able to play an instrument if you wanted to be an idol.

Professional musicians existed merely to be employed. In the beginning these men were renegade jazzers and fugitives from dance bands – hardbitten, professional jongleurs proficient on the electric guitar, the bass fiddle (later electric bass), drums, piano and sometimes saxophone. Trumpeters were not unknown. They backed the earliest rock and roll solo singers with fluency and precision, all toupees and knowing smirks and baggy trousers, doing their bit for posterity in an era when every male over fifteen automatically looked fifty – but even so these pro musicians *were*, quite often, at least that age; and to hear them referred to *en passant*, in vintage rock and roll motion pictures, as 'kids', is still among my keenest pleasures.

The position of *l'artiste* on this question of musicianly skills was markedly different. Quite early on the public latched on to the (generally correct) notion that the guitar-toting idols were merely 'three-chord merchants', i.e. musically unproficient. This was a slightly misplaced jibe, since learning even three chords requires a certain amount of dedication and hard work. But at the same time, for the early rock and roll idols – epitomized by Elvis – the guitar was unashamedly a prop.

There was nothing wrong with this state of affairs. Indeed, it can be said to have been a balanced and healthy attitude to the demarcation of labour. There was mutual respect between the pro musicians and *l'artiste*. It is to be doubted whether Elvis ever instructed his lead guitarist Scotty Moore on the intricacies of the Gm13 chord any more than Moore would have presumed to give El the lowdown on precisely how to scissor his knees on the penultimate line of 'All Shook Up'. The idol was relieved of the burden of having to acquire skills of which he had no real need, and the musicians stayed in work.

But Satan, they say, makes mischief for idol hands. The *modus vivendi* between idol and backing musicians depended on the former's continuing lack of musical ambition – on his ultimate placidity and dimness, one might say, in which category Elvis stands alone. This early, healthy, eminently desirable state of affairs was not fated to last.

We shall never learn which of the Founding Fathers was the first to put his intellect to hitherto unprecedented strain and learn a fourth chord. It is one of those events, like the discovery of fire, which cannot be dated with any precision. By the time of the True Death of Rock and Roll (see chapter 1), there were already quite a few idols capable of playing *at least a dozen different chords, and even the occasional lead break!* The ancient consensus was breaking up.

In many ways this was a touching phenomenon, rather reminiscent of the yokel-betters-himself theme so often found in late-Victorian literature. In some cases it was a perfectly natural response. After all, if one has taken the trouble to learn three chords, why *not* a fourth? Even a fifth! And two or three brace of facile twiddly bits to link them up!

From such seemingly worthy beginnings a curse was unleashed upon unsuspecting humanity: the Guitar Hero experienced his unholy genesis.

It was soon noticed that there was a special cachet attached to guitar-playing skills, a little extra oomph which really added up to a new category of idol. Although the day of the Guitar Hero proper lay still some way in the future, the ability to *play one's own solos* – in fact, to do all one's own lead-guitar work – clearly benefited the idol. On guitar, the very short white man Charlie Gracie (playing a guitar about nine sizes too big for him) and the stringy black man Chuck Berry (who must surely have had the face of a wicked, wicked old man even when he was in his cradle) dominated, though notice was also taken of the clean-cut white guitarist Duane Eddy, who has always refused to sing (what can his voice be *like,* one wonders).

Then there was Buddy Holly, who went one step farther and popularized the styled electric guitar. Up till Holly's time rock and roll guitarists, whether pro back-up musicians or full-blown idols, had always played large 'cello' guitars, designed for portly jazzmen wearing badly tailored jackets to play across the lap while sitting down behind music stands. As their name implies, these instruments are as rotund as the people who play them. They have physical depth, due to the fact that this design of guitar represents a hybrid stage between acoustic and electrically amplified properties. To play them while standing up, even bopping around, is difficult and (*pace* chapter 2) fraught with potential ridiculousness.

The first modification made, therefore, was to slim the instrument down in at least one dimension. The result was the semi-acoustic guitar. This style immediately became (and has remained) popular, but still there was one stage farther to go before wholly unnecessary subtleties like acoustic resonance could be junked and the electric guitar assume its true, lasting, atavistic role as genital extension.

This was the solid-body guitar, an instrument which, as its name implies, has no natural resonance at all, and is merely a sturdy frame on which to hang a fingerboard, electronic pick-ups, and the appropriate number of strings.

They came, and still come, in any number of styles (though fleshy, organic curves have proven most popular) and at all price tags. Indeed they were, and are, an entirely logical development based on the true needs of the guitar-skilled idol. In one way guitars now became more prop-like than ever before; in another they actually became more efficient as musical instruments.

It is a truism – one of the whiskeriest around – that pop guitarists get their jollies from strutting around manipulating gigantic, steel-strung artificial phalli. If the full relentless logic of the Freudian line be followed, this must surely mean that somewhere behind all that glitz and machismo of pop idoldom there must lurk a fairly hefty slice of the old sexual insecurity. Now, you might well exclaim at this point, 'Who is this jerk to point the finger?' – and I do not introduce the subject in order to mock the individuals concerned (not all of whom can be fairly said to have suffered from screaming sexual insecurity). I mention it because it is yet another index of the fraudulence that lay, and lies, behind the rock and roll ethos.

Fraud or not, solid-body guitars caught on. Other instrumentalists did their best to think up ways in which their equipment could be modified. Pianists had the most trouble; the best, by way of outrage, that you can do with a piano (no amount of modification making it portable) is to play it with some bizarre part of your anatomy. Like your feet. Little Richard and Jerry Lee Lewis (again, one black man and one white) went in for this; but the general view seemed to be 'When you've seen one keyboard exponent's crotch you've seen them all.' The elevated-leg style never really caught on.

Bassists had more luck. Formerly, the purveyors of those low, low notes used the double bass, or string bass, or bass (bull) fiddle, largest of the viol family, an instrument which, played wholly pizzicato, derived directly from the preceding jazz era. Here, at least, one can see a case for the invention of a new type of instrument. The string bass has inescapably comic overtones, and the fact that you can actually do quite a lot with it (spin it on its vertical axis, shin up and down it, etc.) did not in any way mitigate the clown-like image most early rock and roll string bassists possessed. So it was no surprise when the bassists turned *en masse* to the more liberating and above all far more phallic bass guitar, which closely resembled the conventional semi-acoustic or solid-body guitar, right down to the rounded curvaceousness of the styling.

Determined not to be left out of this mucho macho, hi-tech, retooling process, drummers – traditionally the dimmest members of any combo – were left with only one practical alternative: increase the number of drums. So began a process which led to the truly monster drumkits of the sixties and early seventies, when gigantism reached the most absurd and terrifying heights, and long, boring drum solos became the rage.

Meanwhile the urge to improve oneself instrumentally was now a runaway train. Increased playing ease and various individual technological improvements (lighter gauge strings, plastic drum heads, superior amplification, tremolo arms, etc.) fed the fires of ambition. Some of the little bastards actually became quite good!

There is something almost Faustian in the way that the actual development of skills, and acquiring of musical knowledge, led directly to – was an integrated part of – the True Death of Rock and Roll. The appeal of the latter had, before the emergence of the virtuoso, lain in simplicity and the good old atavistic surges generated by the sight of a handsome if surly young man of marriageable age warbling manhood songs while simultaneously wobbling his manhood. But the simple, charming, basic appeal of the dim-witted stud consumed with sexual pride began to give way to a more complex assembly of images. No longer was admission restricted exclusively to handsome young studs with nothing between their ears (though they still form a large category of the rock-employed). Ugly young neurotics, some of them quite intelligent, most of them with profound sexual insecurities, became suddenly eligible, on account of their newly acquired musical skills. Neo-primitivism gave way, inevitably, to the Baroque (and later the Rococo), and the clear waters of simple teenage lust were muddied by strange, complex subthemes.

In this large-scale abandonment of a healthy, albeit gormless, barbarism, we see an age-old paradoxical theme in the continuing story of mankind once again taking shape, i.e. that though barbarians, by their vigour, frequently overthrow civilizations, it is the latter who have the last laugh, since the invariable first act of any newly triumphant barbarian is to adopt – wholesale – as many of the attributes of the newly overthrown civilization as he can comprehend.

There was a terrible lesson here for the Founding Fathers but, as has been pointed out, they were mostly too dim to read, and anyway history holds no lessons for the youthfully committed.

Rock and roll died.

Meanwhile, all across the Western world, about a hundred thousand guitarists of differing abilities were quietly practising in front of mirrors.

There now appeared a short *moyen âge*: the Era of the Clean-cut Crooner. A great number of these people were called Bobby. There is absolutely nothing more to say about any of them.

The guitar contingent kept on practising. Some of them – lads who had taken up the instrument in the later fifties – were by now definitely adept in their chosen styles.

For the pro musicians – most of whom, though ageing fast, were still happily in work – it must have seemed as if this Elysian bliss of full employment would go on for ever. Little did they know they were witnessing a *fin de siècle*.

It is difficult to pinpoint with any precision when public interest first switched away from the idol to the group. It is popularly supposed to have happened with the Beatles, but it's my guess that the seeds were sown earlier. As soon as an idol gave a name to his act *which incorporated his backing musicians* (i.e. Freddie Bell and the Bellboys, Buddy Holly and the Crickets) he gave tacit recognition to the fact that there *was* some sort of collective identity to the act. Granted, Freddie Bell could have booted out a Bellboy, Elvis could have junked a Jordanaire and Holly could have croaked a Cricket, and the aforementioned collective identity would have remained intact. In fact, such changes would have received little or no publicity, nor would they have been noticed by any save the fired one and his family. The cornerstone of any act – no matter what its name was – was the idol, and in those days he could damn well do what he liked. At least, his manager-figure could.

But still the collective-identity seed had been sown. In the early sixties it began to flower – if that is the term.

And now, at last, we come to the Beatles.

If anyone doubts that quite enough has been said on the subject of the Beatles in the traditional areas of discussion, let him swing an optic along this:

The wide-eyed, open-eared effects created in Beatle songs by mediant relationships and side-stepping modulations are the empirical product of the movement of melody, modally conceived, and of the behaviour of hands on guitar strings or keyboard. Similar accidents occur in medieval and early Renaissance music, with a comparable synthesis of innocence with sophistication.*

The Beatles have been dissected as a social phenomenon, as composers (see above), as economic entities and as cultural messiahs. They have been biographed, analysed, interviewed, discussed, listed and discographized. One area, however, remains unexplored: *The Beatles' role as disinheritors of the pro musician!*

The Beatles were a group: they are the epitome of the lads we left, back in the late fifties and very early sixties, practising their guitar-playing in front of mirrors. They were not, of course, the only youths so employed. In fact, in the city where they grew up and eventually achieved fame, there were – to my recollection – about sixty thousand similar combos; and quite a few of these – leaving the Beatles aside for a moment – achieved a fleeting fame at a local, regional and (post-Beatles) even national and international level. Therefore it was in the English city of Liverpool that the moving finger wrote its message of doom for the pro musician, and, having writ, moved on.

NO WORK HERE, said the fiery letters on the khazi wall. PISS OFF.

Before long the dole queues of the Western world were swelled by a sudden mass influx of bitter, disgruntled, balding, hard-drinking, middle-aged men carrying trumpets, accordions, etc. Pawn shop windows filled up with any number of overlarge band jackets in tasteless combinations of material and colour scheme. Membership of the Musicians' Union grew mightily – but it was too late. The group format

---

*From *Twilight of the Gods: The Beatles in Retrospect* by Wilfred Mellers (Faber & Faber), 1973.

had arrived – do-it-yourself pop music – and the oldsters were out of a job.

A few found sanctuary doing session work, i.e. impersonating pop musicians in the anonymous conditions of the recording studio. Others reverted to their original line of work (playing in sad six-pieces – weddings, barmitzvahs, etc. – with names like Syd Anthrax and His Sound). A lot packed it in altogether. It was the end of an era – the breaking of a link forged long before in the white heat of Elvis's gyrating trouser seat. Henceforth the new breed was on its own.

Well, not quite on its own, as a matter of fact. I have already mentioned the session men. These tended to be younger (though not always) and more adaptable than the great mass of their contemporaries. Most of them had at least a ten-year start on the new breed – in terms of instrumental expertise – and they put that advantage to good use.

For it turned out, initially at least, that the level of skill deployable by the do-it-yourselfers, while more than adequate in the frenzied and acoustically undemanding confines of the gig, was sometimes not up to scratch in the necessarily more clinical conditions of the recording studio. Deprived of the usual crush of adoring nymphs and hero-worshipping youths, pop groups of the early sixties tended to go to pieces when confronted by cold-eyed A&R men, themselves answerable to giant recording companies, who demanded that tuning be precise, that vocals be intelligible, that amplification be turned *right down*. Even the Beatles' first recording sessions, at EMI studios, were marred. At that time drummer Ringo Starr was a very new addition to the band (the Beatles' first move, on acquiring a recording deal, was to ditch their previous drummer Peter Best), and A&R man George Martin, eyeing the large-nosed, heavily beringed percussionist, was smitten by last-minute doubts. As a result the group's first single 'Love Me Do' – was recorded (in seventeen takes) with a session man called Andy White on drums, while Starr was given a tambourine to rattle. Ah, the dignity of art! The story is that the final, released version was one of those few takes on which Starr *had* actually played the drums (White presumably having had to go for a zizz now and again) – but *my* question is: how do we know this is the case? When you have as many as seventeen different recordings of the same unremarkable song, how can *anybody* say with any certainty which is which? And if they know, why should they tell us the truth? I wouldn't, in their place, if it didn't suit me.

But this intermediate stage did not last – the new breed was getting better and better all the time. Nobody has ever suggested, for example, that any old session man ever substituted for George Harrison's lead guitar parts, or for John Lennon's voice, or Paul McCartney's bass guitar. In fact, said lead guitar, voice and bass guitar were major contributors to the Beatles' collective musical identity. Not only was the group's playing and vocalizing far from incompetent, it was positively pleasing – to millions – and it is safe to say that no session musician on earth (after the 'Love Me Do' affair) could have substituted and got away with it.

This rapidly became true of any number of the better-known groups who staggered to mass popularity in the Beatles' wake. From the point of view of the session man – the rump of pro musicians – now was the time to take the auspices, check out the omens, and start specializing on instruments that pop groups did not play. Like, for example, the violin and other conventional instruments of the symphony orchestra. (Example: the Beatles song 'Yesterday', which features a string quartet.)

But these opportunities were getting fewer and fewer; string orchestra session work is all very well, but considering the average size of a studio string orchestra is at least twenty persons, not many recording budgets allow for them.

Besides, there have always been more than enough violinists, cellists, etc., to go round. Such sessions as were available were rapidly snapped up by these symphonic refugees. It was becoming tougher and tougher for the session musicians.

Then, in the late sixties, there was a scandal of underwhelming proportions when it leaked out that *not one single member* of the Love Affair pop group – who at that time had a substantial hit, 'Everlasting Love' – had in fact played *in any capacity at all* on the recording which bore their name (though it should be made clear that the singer had indeed sung). The national press affected shock, horror, dismay, etc., but the outrage failed to catch fire and the combo went on to a further year or two of moderate success.

Out of near-disaster came a new trend: honesty.

It became the practice to credit, on the sleeves of LPs, each and every session man who had taken a part – be it ne'er so humble – in the recording process. At first this was (one suspects) mere tokenism. Later it became, as so many things do in the wonderful world of rock and roll, a fetish in its own right. Everybody who had even been *in* the studio on the relevant day acquired a printed credit. If they had played an instrument or near-instrument they got a namecheck. If they had supplied tea, cocaine, whisky, etc. they got a namecheck. If no one could actually remember what it was they'd done, they were officially credited for some amorphous service like 'good vibes'. Groups and artistes began to rival each other to see who could credit the largest segment of massed humanity on their LP sleeves. The situation grew to grotesque proportions.

Worse still, from the viewpoint of the genuine session man, the trend towards instrumental competence continued at a breathtaking pace. The standard pop group instrumental ensemble – guitar, electric bass, drums – were the areas in which the pros first felt the pinch. Later, by the mid-sixties, as rock and roll musicians grew competent (relatively speaking) on pianos and organs, these too became areas in which there was no longer any requirement for specialist help. And there was an even grimmer trend shaping up: *pop musicians began to play on each others' recording sessions!*

Luckily there remained – and still remains – one area where the session man, who at the turn of the last decade looked like a highly endangered species, could still make a substantial living: so-called MOR (or 'middle-of-the-road') pop.

In most senses MOR stands for the linear descendants of the Bobbies, the Clean-cut Crooners whose golden age came in between the True Death of Rock and Roll and the emergence of the Group. MOR represents Tin Pan Alley's last beachhead in pop music. For would-be idols, both male and female, continued – and continue – to appear, at astonishingly regular intervals. And while most of them flare and die in barely noticed moments of incandescence (the term 'one-hit wonder' was specifically coined to meet this case), a few actually stick and build careers.

Most importantly, hardly any of them can play a note!

This means work for session men. And unemployment being the red-hot political issue that it is, it can therefore be said that the MOR establishment, which continues to be reasonably productive (in terms of weight, if not quality, of product), is performing a valuable service to the community.

So much for the session men.

We come to the Guitar Hero.

And again we observe one of humanity's seemingly immutable laws in progress. This runs as follows: the urge towards self-improvement, while understandable in the context of near-total ignorance and incompetence, invariably becomes an end in itself and thereby leads to disaster.

Take science. Archimedes invents a device to enable Syracusan peasants to irrigate their vines – and before you know it, you have the fusion bomb, the particle beam weapon and space-based lasers.

It has been the same with rock and roll.

Out of a wholly innocent desire to improve himself – and explore the instrument he is nominally supposed to be playing – a rock idol acquires definite, un-sneerable-at skills on, say, the guitar. Result 1: a load of worthy, conscientious pro musicians are thrown out of gainful employment. Result 2: his music now undergoes deliberate change in order that he can show off his newly acquired expertise. Quite soon, the means have become the end, and all is darkness and sorrow.

Few will argue if I state that the first real Guitar Hero in either hemisphere was Eric Clapton, a skinny, white English youth. Clapton made his name by copying – with dedicated fidelity – the Chicago style. He was closely followed by the American mestizo Jimi Hendrix, who, in terms of originality and musical daring (and sexual imagery) was, and remains, the ultimate exponent of Guitar Hero-dom. But Hendrix died, and Clapton became badly addicted to heroin,* and there the matter should have rested.

But just as Syracusan Archimedes couldn't be content with the water screw (he *had* to go on and invent the fusion bomb), this particular train just kept on rolling. No sooner had Clapton locked himself away in his Surrey mansion with sunglasses, a clean set of 'works' and a suitcase-full of money, than a whole slew of copyists and parallel-developers emerged. A few of them, like the goblin-featured Jeff Beck and the Black Magic aficionado Jimmie Page, were easily as adept as 'God' (Clapton), if not quite in the deceased Hendrix's class. And there were others. It soon turned out that even the ugliest guitarists – many of whom played in small-town, frankly no-hoper groups – were quite capable of 'laying down' convincing impersonations of angst-wracked Chicagoans.

What you needed to do this was (a) a repertoire of blues licks, (b) an electric guitar capable of respectable sostenuto, if possible one of the Gibson range designed by, or signed by, a certain Les Paul, and (c) a fruity, distorted amplifier sound.

Auxiliary assistance was yours in the form of certain electronic devices which appeared on the market at about this time: a fuzz-box (distortion gizmo); a treble booster (or bass-frequency suppressor), a phase pedal (a kind of primitive synthesizer); and other gadgets. Items like the portable echo chamber – which had actually been around for years – now made a comeback.

> With his guitar connected to his
> Fuzz Box
> And his Fuzz Box connected to his
> Tone Pedal
> And his Tone Pedal connected to his
> Treble Boost
> And his Treble Boost connected to his
> Echo Chamber

*He later kicked the habit for good.

And his Echo Chamber connected to his
Marshall Stack
He's ready to play the blues!*

Ah, yes, the Marshall stack! On the face of it, here is an impenetrable bit of insiders' code. The key word here is 'stack', which by the late sixties had become a crisp synonym for grotesquely large numbers of amplifiers and loudspeaker cabinets.

No Guitar Hero felt dressed without his stack. This was the age of gigantism in instrumental equipment, and the modest 50/100-watt Vox amplifiers (albeit 'miked up' through the PA system) of the Beatles and the Animals had finally given way to tower-block-sized assemblages of amplification which formed a backdrop of living sound: delivering, at enormously high volume, the necessary coarseness of tone that blues-influenced Guitar-Hero groups insisted was *à la mode*.

This was the age of the 'heavy' three- or four-piece. The necessary components were (onstage): said amplifier stack, probably manufactured by the Marshall Company of Great Britain (observe how fearlessly I name the guilty men); colossal drumkit, possibly with gongs and tympani; a PA system of epic power; three or four musicians wearing hideously flared trousers (on which more below) and gaily coloured taffeta shirts; and (offstage): lots of road managers (i.e. labourers); one or two manager-figures; vile table manners; a regrettable disrespect for young womanhood; and lots of money.

By now the innocent, wholly respectful Anglo fascination with the Blues had given way to a grosser epoch, in which youths dextrous on solid-body guitars now determinedly mounted a major cultural *coup d'état* against vocalized pop music. That is, vocals were still included, but very much as a second string to the instrumental bow. The first of these 'supergroups' to make it was the Cream, one of whose (three) members was Eric Clapton. There were Marshall stacks, and flared trousers, and gigantic numbers of drums; and lots of frenzied soloing. And – pillock that I am – at the time I, no less than about ten million others, thought it was all simply wonderful.

'Whaaat?' I would exclaim in wholehearted admiration as Clapton strained and soared, practically busting a bollock-string in his not unsuccessful efforts to impersonate a police siren in love. 'Shoot!' I would exclaim, shaking my head bemusedly, as 'Ginger' Baker, the red-haired, indescribably ugly (but flamboyant) drummer, pounded and thundered. And then there was Jack Bruce, perhaps the most hyperactive bassist of all time, and the group's principal vocalist.

They hated each other, of course, like poison, and almost from the word go.

*'The FX Song' © Murray/Tyler, 1974.

Actually, I have a theory about why so many late sixties/early seventies Guitar-Hero 'heavy' combos ended up loathing each other; and it all has to do with flared trousers.

Care to hear it?

Strictly speaking, the subject of 'flares' (or 'loon pants') comes under the heading of ridiculous clothing and thus properly belongs in chapter 2. Yet for me these garments are a major index of the entire loathly vision I am trying to convey. They are a part of my subjective mythology, a card in my personal Major Arcana, a Jungian archetype dream-symbol, one of the stations of the Tyler Qabala. (*'Do not touch the water!' said the Lady Galadriel softly, and Frodo drew back in awe. 'I know what it was you saw, for that is in my mind also,' she said, nodding. 'Loon pants! The Enemy has many weapons . . .'*) In fact, I firmly believe that the cut of late sixties/early seventies pop combos' onstage pantaloons contains a mystical key to the innate fatuousness and dumbo malevolence that, for me, has always underwritten the sharp end of rock and roll.

Consider, if you will, the flared-trouser style. Not the gentle, barely perceptible increase in the calibre of the trouser leg as it approaches the instep (a kind of proportional cheating of the sort used to such tasteful effect by Greek architects of Pericles' time), but – in the case of the Cream's trousers – a sudden, gross, exponential leap in leg width. Tight ('Oooh!') at the crotch and snug at the knees, at ankle level these breeks easily measured a yard from stem to stern. Feet were wholly invisible. At moments of 'excitement' Clapton and his rivals and copyists would brace legs wide apart (cf. the precise angle adopted by drunks urinating against a garage wall), don facial expressions evocative of Christ's on the Cross, cock their guitars at approximately 45 degrees of angle and *get it on* (you know?). What let Clapton and the others down was not so much the getting on, nor even the ridiculously contorted facial expressions – but what befell the flared trousers while the hero held his pose.

It's a subtly visual point and I must explain it as clearly as I can, since so much depends on it.

Each violently flared trouser leg, seen from the front, takes the form of a truncated isosceles triangle.

Now, move the bases of the triangles as far apart as you can while simultaneously retaining the truncated apexes in the same general area.

Although the inner seams remain more or less perpendicular, the outer seams balloon *yet further outwards*, like a multi-petticoated fifties party frock, almost attaining the true horizontal. The eye naturally follows the extreme line – and this, plus the total invisibility of the feet, causes a subjective optical impression that the posing idol's legs are actually braced at an impossible, contortionist, sinew-cracking angle. And one waits for the ping of the buttons, the ripping of cloth and the thud-thud-trickle-trickle as the blues-wailing gonads explode and roll away across the stage towards the peace-sign-making audience, the ultimate rock and roll souvenirs.

Now it is my theory that when members of supergroups of the era wore highly exaggerated flared trousers – as most of them did – they were subjected to wave upon wave of subconscious anxiety thereby. Not all of them were thick, and many of them *must* have known that they were making possibly the greatest single sartorial mistake since the wholesale adoption of the kilt by peoples of proto-Celtic origin. However, onstage (where one does not, as a rule, spend too much time meditating on the cut of one's trousers) they were of course temporarily able to forget the tragicomic proportions of the garments with which they had chosen to adorn their lower limbs.

Then would inevitably come the cardinal instant, the deadly moment of anti-satori. One man would swing eyes left (or right) across the stage in a routine, showbizzy grimace of ain't-we-really-gettin'-it-on good fellowship . . . and lo! There would be his supercolleague, smirking ritually back, possibly bawling 'Yeah!' – *but above all decked out in the most evilly ridiculous, bitterly humiliating pair of trousers on the face of the entire planet!*

Reaction One: My God, I'm in a *band* with this nerd!

Reaction Two: My God, *I* look like that too!

Meanwhile the drummer – who in any case will be the ugliest member of the band – has his shirt off, generously allowing the roadies in charge of the supertrooper spotlights to illuminate every single pustule, blackhead, 'track mark' and skin blemish in the boldest possible relief.

It's my guess that, at this point, massive, traumatic resentment then came flooding in – many bum notes and prolonged hesitations in the guitar solos of the day are, I feel sure, due to sudden off-the-wall revelations of this type striking home in mid-flow.

In circumstances like these, it's not surprising that virtually all combos of this kind either broke up acrimoniously, or came to be notorious for their in-band hostilities and general psychotic behaviour.

The Cream fought each other like bull terriers and broke up, snarling. The Who similarly hit each other at regular intervals – but early on struck on the idea of taking out their loathing on their instruments (and their hotel rooms), and so stayed together. Led Zeppelin's drummer, John Bonham, and their manager-figure, former UK all-in wrestler Peter Grant, were men of violence in every sense of the word – but also directed it outwards. Jimi Hendrix notoriously despised his back-up musicians – then died of vomit asphyxiation after drugging himself unconscious. This deed may have been due to the poor quality of London nightlife, as I flippantly suggested in an earlier chapter, or it *may* have been an accident . . . *or it may have been a longstanding morale problem due to his trousers!* If so, then this must surely be the extremest reaction on record.

With the arrival of the Great Loon Pants* Psychosis, the Guitar Cowboy begins to clip-clop towards his inevitable sunset. Although legions of clone bands had by now appeared (a few are with us to this day), the gargantuism of the whole thing – enormous walls of amplification, way in excess of need; frighteningly prolific metal Triffids replacing the humble Premier drumkit; interminable guitar solos; increasing 'surrealism' (i.e. meaninglessness) of lyrics; ever-escalating ticket prices; ever-louder PA systems; and above all the grotesque, inhuman proportions of the artistes' trousers – all this rampant, Speer-like gigantism suddenly looked . . . rather ridiculous. Embarrassing, even. Where hitherto one had joyously patronized concerts by these people, and worn the attendance badges with pride, suddenly – imperceptibly – one grew evasive, even casually dismissive. While paying lip-service to the Guitar Heroes' pioneering role, one – somehow – found oneself no longer actually *listening* – not very much, anyway – to their records.

Scientists now say that it may have been a giant comet that killed off the dinosaurs. This may or may not be true, but to my mind it was undoubtedly loon pants that sealed the evolutionary doom of the Guitar Hero of rock and roll's very own Jurassic period.

Never underestimate the power of fashion in this racket.

However, whatever may have happened to Guitar Heroes and flared trousers, gigantism did not die.

Audiences had by now become acclimatized to incredible volume, million-dollar arrays of equipment and virtuoso displays. Nevertheless, the guitar, which had ruled the boards unchallenged since the days of the Founding Fathers, was now due to take a sideways step.

The pianoforte, used during the fifties in moderate and downplayed fashion (except by Little Richard, Jerry Lee Lewis and one or two others too obscure to rate a namecheck), had given way by the mid-sixties to the electronic organ.

Hitherto the electrically driven organ had possessed a rather comical geriatric image. For example, if you'd approached a complete stranger (I admit this is wildly hypothetical) and said, 'Electric organ!' he would certainly have replied, possibly after a moment's thought, 'Mighty Würlitzer!' The sound you would both have had in mind would have

*The term 'loon pants' – so apt, so descriptive – appears to have originated with UK mail-order denim companies. Originates from pantaloons, as any fule kno.

been tremulous with vibrato; while, in your minds' eyes, the actual instrument itself would have risen thundering from the pit, every facet of its design living proof that the taste arbiters of the thirties – so successful in other spheres – had obviously been at the fruit punch when they had put together this rig.

But the invention of the Hammond and other 'portable' electronic organs had quietly been changing all this – at least, among the jazz fraternity; and in those far-off days, where jazz instrumentalists led, rock and roll players followed.

I must admit to a soft spot for the great Hammond. Rigged up with a couple of rotating speakers of the type originally patented by the American Leslie Company, the Hammond offers the moderately talentless pianist an unusually easy path to musical apotheosis. In fact, it's hard to think of an instrument on which it's easier to fake it. However, not all organists needed to fake; jazz organists of quality already existed; the gospel subgenre, also well larded with organ material, was plundered for licks; while the rhythm and blues stylists like Booker T. Jones were veritable models of metronomic precision (even if their melodic soloing was a tadzy bit on the limited side).

It's highly difficult to pose properly while playing a keyboard rig (see Foreword). No matter how profound or blues-wailing your musical input, deprived of an ersatz whanger to wave, you're on Mean Street compared with the guitarists. Keyboardists have long grappled with this problem in various ways. Sitting down to play is logical but boring. Standing up is better, unless you happen (like me) to be far too tall to play like this except by adopting a shambling, prehensile crouch. Yet for some time these were the only alternatives – not to be compared, showbizwise, with shirtless drummers kicking over their hi-hats or straddle-flared guitarists, heads thrown back and brutish faces contorted in ham-actor torment. Compared with these gentlemen, the average keyboardist always looked restrained and prissy. He *could* take his shirt off (and some did), or perhaps wave an arm about from time to time, but essentially he was tied to the static tyranny of his engine.

Then the subcult of instrumental destruction broke surface and now organists at least had the option of smashing up the tools of their trade in best pop-art fashion. Trouble was, while a serviceable guitar could be had for £100 or less in those days even the cheapest organ cost vastly more than that. But one man stood alone, boldly defying the laws of economics: Keith Emerson. This keyboard exponent first came to the British public's attention with his combo The Nice. At the climax of his act Emerson would rock his trusty Hammond L100 to and fro, making the reverberator crash and boom like the sound effects which Fundamentalists assure us will accompany the Day of Judgement. Then he would jump on top of it, the knobbly, unremarkable Englishness of his face dramatically at odds with the piratical *braggadocio* of his pose. Then he would kick it around the stage, rock it right over on to its back, and finally thrust a dirty great chiv between the keys, thus jamming down a vile discord. All this was timed to culminate with the climax of the piece – a version of the US college-jazzer Dave Brubeck's 'Blue Rondo à la Turk' (the knife-wielding Emerson presumably symbolizing Ottoman brutality). This performance was undeniably effective. The term 'rock theatre', much abused then and since, in this case almost fits. So naturally Emerson dumped The Nice and went on to form a new kind of supergroup altogether, the keyboards-led Emerson, Lake and Palmer.

Though in one respect this was clearly a Rococo variant of the loon-panted heavy guitar trio, Emerson had clearly managed to interest one of the more prosperous merchant banks to invest, since the lad was surrounded on three sides by the very last word in up-market, high-tech keyboard instrumentation. Rock and roll gigantism had now invaded the stronghold of Chopin, Lizst and that gentle mystic, Ravel.

There was a grand piano, tuned to within an inch of its life, for Keith to play his classical bit on.

There was a huge Hammond B3 for Keith to play his other stuff on.

There was an old, battered and much stabbed Hammond L100, for Keith to play 'Rondo' on.

And there was a Moog synthesizer.

Microchips have now become so small, compact and powerful and music synthesizers have accordingly become so petite, totally versatile, easy to operate and cheap, that young 'uns tend to forget that, not so long ago, in the very early seventies when technoflash combos of rock virtuosi like Emerson, Lake and Palmer, Deep Purple and The Yes first appeared, the average synthesizer – and Moog, pronounced *Mohg*, was the name of power in this context – was a device closely resembling, and about the size of, a working telephone exchange in a medium-sized industrial town. The full Moog rig, which Emerson of course possessed, was a vast nightmare of sockets, jackplugs, knobs and switches. Yet with all this complexity – which not even its inventor can properly have understood – the damn thing was *monophonic*! That is, it wouldn't play chords, just single notes. So if it was rich in potential, practically and musically, it was of considerably less use than a peg-legged sea rover's salt-stained concertina, properly miked up. And at the volume which Emerson employed, virtually every 'voice' he was able to extract – by means of endless, solemn, tedious patching – sounded like the same old combination of Gideon's trumpet and the 4.44 from Paddington coming through Critchley tunnel with its steam whistle jammed. In fact the only use that Emerson was able to get from his two storeys of Moog synthesizer that he couldn't have got – with knives or even Prussian duelling sabres – from his L100 was a piercing glissando which he modulated by wiping a ribbon-controller device along the groove between his buttocks. (Little did the members of the combo know that some members of the road crew secretly referred to this regular feature of the act as 'Keith sandpapering his haemorrhoids'.)

The E, L & P experience was a prototype in many ways – though it derived from the immediately preceding Guitar Hero *danse macabre avec pantalons du pierrot* period. Others now took this selfsame road. Deep Purple hedged their bets and gave equal prominence to a guitar gonzo and a Hammond ham. The third major UK band to make a splash in this particular area were The Yes.

Here the cult of musicianship was taken to a refined pitch of worthiness, exactly reproducing the atmosphere of exalted boredom that one finds in most state-funded institutions that teach conventional music. Wholly absent from the repertoire of The Yes were the thunderous fortissimos, the hacking and kicking of inoffensive electronic equipment and the bum-wiping that characterized E, L & P. In their place, the gentle, committed artistes of The Yes gave us crescendo and diminuendo plus an ability to play both counterpoint *and* in unison. The Yes positively delighted in producing compositions arranged with near-symphonic (i.e. fanatical) attention to detail. For example, if Bloke A was required, at Spot B, to play seventeen chromatically ascending chords beginning with Zmj7 and ending, precisely seven point six seconds later, with a *ritenuto* on Y diminished, that is what Bloke A did. You could set your watch by him.

They called it 'symphonic rock'.

It was also called 'classical rock' and, in a more unkind sense, 'technoflash'. The whole aura of The Yes's operation was calculated to elevate rock music (note: in those days *not* rock and roll) to a loftier plane, a beatific level where the long-haired git of malevolent public legend could finally, unarguably, be seen to have achieved his long-postponed (but rightful) apotheosis and put himself on an equal footing with . . . well, if not Ludwig Van, then at least Mendelssohn, certainly Brahms and (at a pinch) the late pan-German romantics like Mahler and Strauss (R.).

In other words, the whole symphonic rock thing, exemplified in their different ways by The Yes, Deep Purple and Emerson, Lake and Palmer – but copied, as the Guitar-Hero groups had been, by thousands of lesser acolytes – was another complete betrayal of the simple, loins-based, nonsense-rhyme rock and roll of the Founding Fathers. It was even a betrayal of the modest, if conformist, ambitions of the

Bobbies and all other MOR acts. It was a betrayal of the likeable pop gormlessness of the early Beatles. There is hardly anybody who has ever been associated with rock and roll who was not betrayed – sold down the bloody river – by symphonic rock, which had nothing whatever to do with happy-go-lucky mating calls and sexual display, and everything to do with a permanent and seemingly ineradicable feature of Western – especially English – life: the deadly, dreary urge to be a culture vulture.

There was no denying the technical adeptness of the individual members of The Yes. So obviously in love with their own expertise were they that before long it became clear that they too had fallen into an old, old trap. Their songs (what am I talking about, songs? Their *works*) had clearly been thought up *principally in order to give each individual instrumentalist a fair apportionment of show-off bits*. Ensemble work consisted of meaningless progressions of very difficult chords (that no pukey guitar-picker would ever stumble across in ten years of simple blues-wailing), linked together with endless strings of incredibly demanding arpeggios, the whole punctuated by preplanned if vacuous moments of 'expression'. (Drummer hits cymbal softly with paint brush; sixteen seconds' silence; he hits it again; spotlight on guitarist, who now starts improvised cadenza; band leave stage for a zizz and a quick orange juice.) The entire random set of bits would be linked together by a recurring theme of the utmost blandness, inverted and reprised *ad infinitum* not to mention *nauseam*.

Meanwhile the vocalist – who had a very high voice indeed, making Neil Young sound like a blue-chinned barbershop bassman by comparison – dutifully stood around robed in druidical white, and stepped solemnly forward every now and again to make his own contribution.

Their long-players had titles like *Tales From Topographic Oceans*.

The Yes also had a famous keyboard player of their own – Rick Wakeman, a burly, blond, affable but coarse player of Liberace standard, who to this day holds the all-time record for equipment overkill. If memory serves, Wakeman had (a) a grand piano, (b) an electric piano, (c) a Hammond organ, (d) a string synthesizer, (e) another synthesizer and (f) a Mellotron.

He arranged these things in a three-sided box, with the grand on one side with the electric piano on top of it, the Mellotron on another with a string synthesizer on top of *that*, and, on the third side, his Hammond with another synthesizer on top. Three ranks in hollow square, like a drumming-out ceremony in a French colonial regiment. No less than seven separate keyboards (or 'manuals' as we organists say).

In the middle of all this money stood Wakeman, wearing a silver lamé cloak.

Emerson and his thigh boots and his Moog telephone exchange and his haemorrhoid-sandpapering were shown up, by comparison, as coarse and unrefined.

I should explain this strange word *Mellotron*. This was a hybrid keyboard instrument designed and built in the UK and much favoured for a few years by 'art' bands of the general type we have been discussing. A Mellotron was actually a mechanical monstrosity, virtually a huge multi-decked tape recorder. Press a key – any key, black or white – and you activated a pre-recorded tape loop, one loop for each key. Needless to say, there were lots of moving parts to go wrong. Their chief function was to simulate string instruments; they had an unmistakeable, icy tone, were nevertheless fully polyphonic – and extremely heavy. The advent of the microprocessor-driven string synthesizer dealt this curious contraption's long-term commercial chances a death blow. Nowadays few remain, and those you see and hear are used primarily for their distinctive 'Mellotron' sound.

Technoflash died – almost. E, L & P got grossly rich (and gross) and split up. Deep Purple got grossly rich – and split up. The Yes got grossly rich – and stayed together. After all, it was well known that they were in it for 'the music' as much as anything else. This, despite losing Wakeman for a time; he had career plans all his own, which involved the full assembly of keyboards as well as (regrettably) the silver lamé cloak. (They replaced Wakeman with a Swiss chap called Patrick Moraz who failed to work out long term. Then they brought back Wakeman. Then they settled on someone called Vangelis.) So in The Yes and Barclay James Harvest and a number of other combos symphonic rock lives on, after a fashion, having duly taken its accorded place – along with skiffle, early rock and roll, mod music, Tamla Motown, soul music, Acid Rock, Mersey Beat, protest songs and Heavy Metal – in the ever-proliferating number of sinister tableaux in our imaginary waxworks. For no style ever quite disappears. Walk, trembling and retching, down the dimly lit central corridor of the waxworks and they leer at you from either side, fixed, unmoving, lurid, undead. It's awful.

The excesses of technoflash and symphonic rock led to the New Wave. Like every single movement in the rock and roll story other than the original one, this first took mass-culture form in Britain. It was as reactionary as any of its predecessors, being forged in an understandable desire to be as unlike the preceding wave (i.e. symphonic rockers) as possible. Where the last lot had emphasized 'beautiful' imagery, technical skills and a high investment in equipment, the New Wavers – soon known as 'punks' – clearly made a collective decision to do precisely the opposite. Their imagery was brutal and disgusting – the more so the better. Their technical skills were nil – the idea presumably being to display contempt for any of the orthodox routes to success. This allowed equipment to be as primitive and cheap as possible.

Of course, what was really happening was that a new generation of unmated males was making its takeover bid – any ethologist worth his diploma would have no difficulty whatsoever in drawing a reasonable parallel between the anger and contempt felt by the New Wavers towards their elders, and the behaviour of young male cockroaches at certain times of the year. I have no doubt it would displease the New Wavers of the time greatly to learn that in challenging their peers in this way they were merely obeying the same kind of inner call that activates a juvenile boy cockroach, but none the less it's true.

However, to be fair, there *was* another angle; a particularly British one. The question of class.

At this point I must address my American readers. You may, or you may not, have at some time absorbed an explanation of the British class system, and as a result you may think you understand it – at least, enough to be getting on with. Forget it – there's no way you can even come close to comprehending it. It's too ancient, too arcane, too buried under layers of misunderstanding and antagonism (and mutual respect in surprising doses) even to be understood by its principal beneficiaries and victims. So in explaining the blood feud between the punk rockers and their predecessors (for whom they coined the term 'boring old farts') I can only say – and hope you understand – that, whatever else it was, it was also a new form of the ancient rivalry between the lower order and the middle class.

Like all generalizations, this one suffers when you put it under the microscope. By no means all symphonic rockers and technoflash kids were middle class – drummers, for example, still contained a very high proportion of the sons of the blue-collared. Neither is it true that all punk rockers were barefoot cockneys brought up on a diet of margarine and broken glass. What *is* true is that, by definition, symphonic rockers *taken in the mass* did convey a middle-class aura; there was an uneasy element of Hampstead-style culture present; that nobody can deny. It was also true that – following the principles of blind reaction already described – the New Wavers, whatever their origins, did as much as possible to eradicate, in a kind of mass Maoist cultural revolution, any trace whatever of bourgeois ancestry and upbringing.

They did this is order to seem as unlike the preceding genteel wave as possible. A popular device was the changing of one's name, preferably to something revolting. Johnny Rotten. Sid Vicious. Rat Scabies. . . . Another favoured method was the composing, and performing, of lyrics that – once you'd penetrated them – identified as closely as possible with the supposed interests of working-class British youth.

In fact, they were reincarnations of that fifties literary term, 'Angry Young Men'. They were angry. They fancied themselves as anarchic. And they were – the whole point of the exercise – successful. The Sex Pistols were the supreme example, but there were others. The chief manipulator of this brief fashion was the British entrepreneur Malcolm McLaren, and the number one casualty was the unspeakable Sid Vicious. But there's only so far you can go on a platform of sheer horribleness, and John Lydon, alias Rotten, realized this moderately early on. Besides, an earlier phenomenon was making a reappearance: the punk rockers, after six months of tuneless bashing, had got fed up and learned a few chords. Punk rock gave way to a whole quiverful of new styles – New Romantics, New Psychedelics, etc., none of them individually meaning very much, though collectively they added up to a genuine New Wave – if by New Wave you mean several old waves resuscitated. And once again prominent in British pop music was our old pal, instrumental pretension.

This time it took a wholly reactionary form: it was a response to technology, nothing more and certainly nothing less.

Remember our old friend the Moog synthesizer? Well, while the symphonic types were fighting and losing their battle with the Huns of the day – the punk rockers – across the oceans quiet, competent little men with prominent teeth, short sight and a habit of bumping themselves off if they were late for work more than three times a month, were getting on with a refinement process. Using newly developed microprocessor technology, they first made these machines rather smaller than their predecessors. Secondly, they made them capable of playing chords. Finally realizing that musicians onstage do not have either the time or the inclination to solve problems of exponential resistance – or analyse wave-form structure – before selecting a sound, they replaced the original telephone exchange of plugs and sockets with a handy series of switches and sliders, clearly and conventionally labelled. The result was the new model synthesizer, a compact, versatile instrument capable of simulating an entire string orchestra at the very least.

They can do more than this. The makers had taken the rhythm-box idea from the electronic-organ people of the sixties and integrated their (far superior) versions into their slick, compact, easy-to-use machines.

To be fair, when rhythm boxes first appeared as built-in parts of electronic organs, they were scorned by the rock and roll musicians of the day (to the relief of the drummer fraternity). Essentially they were, and are, gadgets which the 'player' can preset to produce a simulation of drums, and were designed for the home-organ market. In a word, they were electronic metronomes with variable tone. The modern versions of these gadgets – and almost all professional synthesizers have one – are fully capable of replacing drummers – although this latter class, of legendary truculence, made a fight of it, as one might have expected. As a result ultra-modern rhythm boxes now come equipped with thump-sensitive rubber pads which allow, to use the jargon for a moment, a real-time input to interface with the program.

When these widgets first appeared musicianly morale was at an all-time low, thanks to the Neo-Visigoths with barbed wire through their noses who then infested the scene. My personal guess is that 1977 was a quietish year for synthesizer salesmen. Then – as was inevitable – the terrible, raging lust to acquire musical competence once again raised its *arriviste* head and swallowed all the electronic keyboards the super-efficient factories of the Greater Southeast Asia Co-prosperity Sphere could produce.

So was born 'robot music', originally exemplified in Britain by Gary Numan, who, having all his short life so far wanted to be David Bowie, now decided he wanted to be an android. His entire style, like that of Jackie Dennis, was based around a single premise. You set your keyboard, or ensemble of keyboards, to play all by themselves – jerky, fully automated notes in programmed sequence; the old-style rhythm box integrated into the melodic function of the gadget. Then you sang along with the bits and bytes, preferably with your face painted eerily, and with your body swinging in a series of supposedly mechanical jerks. That's all there was to it, and Numan was certainly accomplished enough to make quite a lot of money before his fifteen minutes were up. Like every other style, this one is with us still; a wholly reactionary, thoroughgoing, willing enslavement to the microprocessor. Yet again means have become an end.

Not only that, but in the process the whole dreary cycle has been given a new shot in the arm and as a result has once again been rescued from the oblivion its extreme senility and utter debasement must surely have earned. And just when I thought it was at last going to sag to its knees and expire. It only goes to show how wrong you can be.

But if it *had* expired, I wouldn't be writing this book!

They say every cloud has a silver lining.

SIX

THE BIZ

I was once on television.

It's not every day one finds oneself on television. In fact, in my case it's not *any* day – apart from this one occurrence, which I am about to relate.

Having seen myself on television, I am convinced that this is just as well.

'Ah!' said my editor-figure, bursting into my sordid little cubbyhole one morning and catching me in the middle of a particularly absorbing nose-picking session (it had been a heavy night). 'ITN are on the phone. They want someone to go on "News at One" and talk about corruption in the music business. You go.'

I was not quite sure what he meant by this but who, never having been on television, could pass up the opportunity? Suddenly infinitely desirous of being on television, I cabbed over to Independent Television News – and presented myself to the appropriate authorities.

That very morning, it seemed, the early papers had carried a vague but potentially fruity story involving the BBC, payola, and sex-for-favours. Not to mention hard cash transactions, and the juiciest hint of illicit muscle. This all apparently centred around pop music. Further details were not forthcoming, and as a result ITN had decided to cover the story in the only way left open to them – by hauling in an 'expert' to sound off on the general picture.

Expert? On corruption in the music business? With hindsight it is plain that I should not have allowed my joy at the thought of being on television to override the commonsense notion that this role was not altogether one an aspiring careerist might wish to adopt. Especially since in my case the careerist, in his general appearance, resembled nothing so much as an Oxfam shop. My worst enemies wouldn't accuse me of being well dressed at the best of times and the heavy night had left its toll.

They took me to a hospitality suite and the gopher, observing my wan and seedy condition with ill-concealed disquiet, offered me a generous slug of the most appalling cheap brandy I have ever swallowed. There was some muttering in a corridor, and the producer shoved his head round, smiled anxiously, said, 'All right?' as if he could hardly believe I would have the cheek to answer 'Yes'; and within six or seven minutes (this was at about 11.30 a.m.) I was being shepherded into an enormous, dark cavern. A cathedral-like hush prevailed, and the sacerdotal atmosphere was sharply increased by the glimpses of tiny, twinkling, faraway, coloured lights; and even more by the sense of there being actually rather a lot of people out there in the warm darkness, each quietly absorbed in some private sin. It was intimidating to a degree.

Seated at an enormous padded desk in the only patch of light was a diminutive figure almost submerged under a disproportionately large amount of silver hair. Underneath the silver quiff were the features of the well-known broadcaster Robert Kee. This was not the actual 'News at One' – not unsurprisingly, this goes out at 1 p.m. – but a prerecording of the corruption piece. I have since learned that one of the reasons for prerecording interviews such as this, when 'experts' have to make do instead of news, is that they can be junked, even at the last minute, if something better should come along. At the time, transfixed with rapture at being on television, though simultaneously terrified by the studio atmosphere, I did not know or care.

The enormous desk was vaguely horseshoe-shaped, and as I was seated some considerable distance from Robert Kee I was actually halfway around a sort of corner – which was a little disconcerting. The heat from the studio lights was making me acutely aware of every blemish in my appearance: the unshaven chin, the bloodshot eyes, the greasy skin, the matted hair, the repellent shirt and the dreadful leather jacket which I had bought in Chelsea five years before for £25 and which had never been anything other than an absolute disaster in its own right.

The interview itself passed with blinding speed; I have little memory of it. The producer told me that Robert would be asking me some questions, and to look at him, not at the camera (invisible in the darkness beyond the glare). Robert Kee nodded coldly to emphasize this latter directive. Then authoritative voices came across with the expected jargon ('Quiet, studio!', etc.), and the thing was done.

They hustled me out and shoved me into a taxi with indecent haste, with promises of money to come. I just had time to get home to see myself on television. The taximan obviously recognized this urgency of manner as something often encountered in pick-ups from the ITN building, and bore me along with excellent efficiency. I arrived just before one and switched on the television.

Moments passed, 'News at One' began, and there was silver-haired Robert Kee himself – *with whom I had been sitting not a hour earlier* – burbling along about news stories of infuriating non-importance. Then he paused, looked sadder than usual, and said: 'Allegations over a corruption ring at the BBC involving sex for payment and other practices were made today by . . .' and I leaned forward, elbows tight into my sides at my eagerness to see myself on television.

And suddenly there I was – on television! Captioned, yet! Looking ill and shifty, and seedy and corrupt, and altogether loathsome. Off-camera, Robert Kee's voice came over suavely. 'Tony Tyler!' he said. '*Is* there a great deal of corruption in the music business?'

The wretched, tortured interrogatee writhed under the spotlight. His eyes flickered nervously to and fro and his evil leather coat creaked foolishly.

'Er – not a lot. No,' he replied, the epitome of guilty defensiveness.

My stomach turned to water at the hideous stupidity of my agreeing to appear at all. But I had been blinded by vanity and the lust to be seen – just once – on television.

Kee got absolutely nothing out of me. (I was barely able to comprehend my own speech.) What did emerge were a few muttered sentences, banal in the extreme, about 'lures' and 'temptations'. Now visibly in despair, Kee asked: 'But do you yourself have any experience of bribery or anything like that?' – and by the upwards rolling lurch of his interviewee's eyeballs you could see, plain as a pikestaff, that his interviewee most definitely had. 'Er . . . no,' he croaked, and that was that. He vanished from the nation's screens. For ever.

I was forced to admit that whatever else could be said against the item from a personal viewpoint, its hard news value was not exactly riveting either. By early evening my one and only appearance on television had been dropped from the ITN broadcast in favour of a slightly less feeble version of the same thing done by somebody else.

I did not go back to work that day; and I debated earnestly with myself whether to go to work the following day either (or ever again, for that matter). But that day was a Black Tuesday, when the magazine was printed, and here was one duty I could not dodge, being responsible for one or two of the most drab and downbeat sections of the journal. Armoured against inevitable scorn, I went to the printers.

My teeth-gritting was unexpectedly rewarded. None of my colleagues mocked my appearance on 'News at One' for the very good reason that none of them had seen it! With them, therefore, I was able to be bluff and dismissive, leaving the impression that, in its own way, my television debut had been something of a minor *chef-d'oeuvre*. But in my heart I knew there was still the composing-room crew to face. They worked shifts, and as a result at least *some* of them must surely have viewed the previous day's 'News at One'.

Sooner or later I knew I had to emerge from the comparative safety of the journalists' quarters and saunter around the composing room, to check the progress (or otherwise) of 'my' pages. As nonchalantly as possible – and fully aware that my escape hitherto could now only be karmically balanced by a prolonged nightmare of jeering humiliation at the hands of these notoriously outspoken men – I went out to meet my fate.

An aged comp spotted me the instant I emerged. He nudged a withered companion, and both of them advanced purposefully. Here it comes, I thought, and switched on my martyr's smile as they approached. In my mind I was already practising the rueful chuckle and the words of amused self-deprecation ('Yes, it *was* rather ghastly, wasn't it?') that I had already decided were my only viable form of self-defence. (The ability to manifest apparent gentle pleasure at one's own hideous pratfalls is one of life's more useful secrets.)

''Ere!' said the aged comp, confronting me; his pal was a yard or two behind. 'Didn't I see you on television yesterday?' I acknowledged that he had probably done so and waited resignedly. He kept me in suspense by first turning to his pal and saying 'I told you it was 'im, didn't I?' Then he turned back to me.

' "News at One", wernit?'

Again I nodded.

His face split into a broad smile. 'Well, I'm buggered,' he theorized. 'I *thought* it was you!' With that he and his friend turned and walked away, chattering excitedly. It now became apparent that the fact that my one and only appearance on television had been a sorry debacle was altogether obscured from their sight. For them, it was enough that someone with whom they had the briefest of professional acquaintance had *actually been on television*! The quality or otherwise of his performance was utterly irrelevant in the far stronger light of their knowing, in person, a bloke who had, the day before, been on television.

For the rest of that miraculous day I basked in an all-round glow of admiration. None of the other print-room staff had chanced to see me and as a result their view of this event was entirely shaped by the substance of the aged compositor's excited tale-spreading. For the rest of the day I was followed, wherever I went, by admiring glances, knowledgeable nods, and the oft-repeated whisper ''E was on television!'

It wasn't until quite a bit afterwards that I took the trouble to find out what the corruption story had been all about.

It turned out that it *had*, after all, been about the BBC and sex-for-favours and crooked record-plugging. One or two people got medium-term prison sentences . . . and then the story died.

The reason it died, just like that, is that the news media lost interest the very minute the judge had taken off the black cap and the newly convicted had been led away to the cells. And the reason they lost interest is because every news professional worth his salt knows that people *expect* the music business to be corrupt, just as they expect the art world to be peopled largely by androgynes. It excites no comment, and is therefore death to newsmen. When the public *do* get excited is when a pillar of rectitude gets it on the neck – when a vicar interferes with choirboys, for example, or a well-known campaigner against loose public morals is found in a Soho dive wearing a maid's uniform, or – sorry, Mr President – when a right-wing politician gets involved in chicanery and fails to cover his arse properly. They are merely bored when a member of what is popularly seen as a dissolute elite behaves in a dissolute fashion. This, despite the public's fascination with appearances on television of members of that elite.

The denizens of the wonderful world of rock have not been backward in providing bitter criticism, over the last ten years or so, of the way their industry works. The realization that the music biz, like many another biz, has sharks in its pool coincided with the discovery – by late twentieth-century Americans – of economics theories which, in 1865, were the last word in progressive thinking; and many a rip-off has been exegesized since that time.

Unfortunately a slightly uncertain note is struck by the fact that, whenever music writers expose a rock and roll business scandal, they seldom if ever do so in their parent magazines, or indeed for any magazine. Real scam is usually worth a paperback book contract, at the least; sometimes a story such as this might be handed over *in toto* to a real newspaper, who naturally appoint their own staffers to check it out and write it all over again. This tends to rob music papers of that crusading image they would do well to acquire.

Another peculiarity of rock and roll exposés is that they seldom, if ever, occur (that is, the exposés) while the alleged rip-off is *actually taking place*. This is partly because of the threat of a libel action (which all writers should bear constantly in mind); another reason is that music writers are not professionally tooled up to mount such investigative journalist's projects. A third, most cogent of all, is that one doesn't tend to find out that a rip-off or scam has been taking place until some time after it is over, when the more disgruntled party blows the whistle and shleps the whole shebang into court.

The two most celebrated (alleged) rip-offs in the history of rock and roll centre around its two most famous acts ever, Elvis Presley and the Beatles. In the former case, the lawsuits and the bitter allegations involve the financial relationship between (1) Elvis, (2) the dead Elvis, and (3) 'Colonel' Tom Parker, Presley's lifetime manager-figure. In a nutshell: since the party of the first part can no longer testify, a faction representing the party of the second part is making life difficult for the party of the third part, alleging that the relationship between the party of the third part and the party of the first part (on the one hand), and the party of the third part with the party of the second part (on the other hand) was (and is) grossly unfair, being absurdly loaded in favour of the party of the third part in both instances. Meanwhile the party of the third part is counter-suing vigorously, alleging precisely the opposite. The case may well reach the Supreme Court by the turn of the next century – by which time, 'Colonel' Tom Parker's years being as advanced as they are, we may well be treated to the comparatively rare spectacle of two deceased persons suing each other for amounts of money which by then will total billions of dollars.

The second famed contretemps is far more complicated than the relatively simple quarrel about bucks which currently divides Tom Parker and Presley's estate. The truth is that the Beatles were always appallingly managed: a great deal of the complication in their business affairs derives from the period *before* the setting-up of the ill-fated Apple company. It now appears – though we didn't hear this at the time – that during Brian Epstein's stewardship of his boys, virtually *anybody* could walk into NEMS and walk out with some kind of exclusive marketing franchise – for which the Beatles themselves rarely saw a cent.

But the Epstein period, in terms of incompetence and sheer green-hornism, was *as nothing* to the period which followed his death, when the group for a while pretended to manage their own affairs, jointly, in the name of their purpose-formed company, Apple.

Since the story has been told many times at considerable length, the best short description of Apple is 'an organization for giving away money'; to which must be added, damning though it is, 'inefficiently'. The four idiots from Merseyside, full to the gills (and who wasn't in those days?) with various pleasant, non-addictive intoxicants, wrote their company's memorandum of association in a spirit of matchless gonzo wholly appropriate to the times. The result was that every sharp, twister, 'ligger', mouth-artist, groupie and earnest hippie seeker after knowledge for miles converged on the company's Savile Row HQ and started, slowly at first and then with accelerating speed as the unbelievable facts sank in, to remove property and cash, often in considerable amounts.

To be fair, the Beatles had always *intended* to give away money –

but in the form of investment 'to get people started', to uncork the supposedly bottomless well of spirit renaissance which the jasmine-flavoured attitudes of the sixties – and the Beatles themselves – had so effectively provided. In fact, money and property were simply *taken*, quite unaccountably, and not by people of talent, but by people with light fingers; *not* quite the class of creative genii the Moptops had presumably had in mind.

Cadgers descended on Savile Row in company strength. The word was, if somehow you could get *in*, you could count on getting *out* afterwards *with* something; a cheque, an executive toy, a silver disc, a few old master tapes . . . even an ashtray would do.* Before long Apple had virtually ceased trading altogether. Only its record division continued to maintain a ghostly presence. The lads had departed – in four different directions.

There then followed a protracted series of continuing arguments over money and manager-figures. By this time the two richest Beatles – by virtue of their songwriting – were John Lennon and Paul McCartney. These two each separately advanced two protégés, one masculine candidate for the job of Beatles manager, plus one feminine candidate for the scarcely less demanding role of life's partner. It was McCartney (who seems to have taken the better advice), who later brought a contentious High Court action to have the Beatles, as a company, officially terminated. This was partly to do with his fierce dislike and mistrust of New York businessman Allen Klein. John Lennon had been instrumental in involving Klein's ABCO company in Apple's affairs – especially once these were seen to have degenerated to fiasco level. Klein is everyman's idea of a music businessman: he looks the part, even. His initial role was to rationalize the demise of Apple Corps. He did so double quick, but then showed unmistakable signs of wanting to make his commanding role permanent: in other words, to replace Brian Epstein. This, Lennon was apparently more than willing to countenance – it was McCartney who gave Klein the low sign. Soon, he was promoting his own manager candidate; his new father-in-law, another New York businessman, John Eastman.

In the event each of the senior Beatles scored only a 50 per cent victory. Each won the girl of his heart but utterly failed to foist the manager-figure of his dreams on the other co-equal compadre. Result: a classic decoalescence situation.

For rather than submit to a *pax kleini*, McCartney wound up the

---

*Shortly before this book was published, I was describing its contents to a friend of mine, a successful director of pop videos. When I got to the Apple bit he said. 'Ah yes, I was one of the Apple scruffs . . . I got some great early photographs from a filing cabinet which had been left open and unattended . . . still got them somewhere.'

Beatles altogether. The entire assets of the Beatles hitherto were officially frozen by the presiding High Court judge. Boy, was McCartney popular!

Lennon hated him for (a) hurtfully not taking his advice over Allen Klein, (b) breaking up the Beatles, and (c) making a balls of (b) so that the cash was placed beyond reach.

George Harrison hated McCartney for (a) being bossy in the studio, and (b) breaking up the Beatles.

A lot of fans, having got over the recent rumour of McCartney's 'death', hated him in droves simply for breaking up the Beatles.

It's fairly safe to assume he wasn't that popular with Allen Klein, either.

In a superb and gentlemanly spirit of loyalty to his protégé, Lennon immediately declared his abiding faith in Allen Klein, and declared that *his* affairs, at least, would continue under ABCO's benign and wholly efficient stewardship.

Three years later he was suing Klein's arse into the ground.

It now becomes necessary to define the music business and the way it works.

The well of all bounty is the general public. Without them, nothing. Parting the pop public from its geld is the number one priority of 99 per cent of all those who are counted part of the 'biz'.

There are two ways of doing this. One is to persuade the pop public to buy records; the other is to inveigle them into attending concerts and personal appearances. Despite the apparent competition between these two forces, in reality they exist in a near-perfect symbiosis and each has the effect of increasing the other's take. Records sell concert tickets, and all but the most disastrous concerts increase the sales of records.

Taking record companies first, they acquire revenue from direct sales of records. Against that they must set their total overheads, including manufacture, distribution and advertising, the publishing monies, and the performer's royalty. If they know their job – and many do – they are still left with a sizeable 'drink' at the end of the day.

The major risk they take is self-evident: signing a 'turkey', or (worse) a soon-to-be 'turkey', whose records not only fail to sell, but cost the earth to produce and manufacture, distribute, etc. If the said turkey has meanwhile wrung millions of dollars from the record company in one form or another (see below), major loss can loom on the horizon. Just as record companies have been known to come into existence on the strength of one major long-playing success (e.g. the UK Virgin Record's *Tubular Bells*), so other record companies have been near-bankrupted by a single, colossal failure. A string of unwise signings can send them out of business. So their first priority – is self-defence, you can understand – is to screw down on the screwable areas right from the start. They have no incentive to be overgenerous, any more than any other business operation.

Where concerts are concerned the record companies can only stand on the sidelines, since this time the take is shared between the promoter or impresario – the producer of the event, who bears all expenses – and the artiste or act. The proportion of the take received by the act depends on the inherent fame and earning power of the headliners themselves.

There are even finer distinctions separating megastars from mere superstar acts. The latter are content to take a hefty slice of the net and accept less overall money in return for less of a risk. Real big deals go for a piece of the gross. They *know* there is no real risk involved and they also often impose upon the poor promoter (and after he's finished dipping into his wallet he *is* poor) contractual conditions so absurdly swingeing, so gross, and so mischievous, that, reading them, one can only guess that they have been deliberately concocted, in a mass, malicious 'Let's-stitch-up-old-Harvey' spirit.

Promoters take more conventional risks too. One of the greater fiascos of my day was the so-called Great Western Festival, held near the easterly British town of Lincoln in 1972. This was bang slap in the middle of the early seventies pop festival craze and was, in terms of sheer scale and trouble taken to provide a balanced range of activities, easily the most gigantic British effort yet. It became widely known that the event was being staged by a consortium of British businessmen (not music biz types at all), fronted by the well-known film actor Stanley Baker (since deceased), famous in his time for playing gritty-jawed paranoids.

The Great Western Festival was fixed for midsummer. Everything had been thought of; even a site had been found, miles out in the Lincolnshire fens, far away from cottagers who might complain. Car parking had been laid on, and toilets. There would be hot-air balloons and carnival attractions; all kinds of food, day or night; places to wash and sleep; plus five days of non-stop rock and roll, each day capped with six or seven acts of considerable, if not excessive, earning power and fame. The press facilities were to be a model of their kind. Security would be first class. It was all going to be absolutely wonderful.

There was an ominous portent when, a few weeks earlier, the first of that year's British cash-ins on the festival boom, the event staged at Bickershaw, Lancashire, was destroyed by torrential rain. I attended both festivals (in my professional capacity, of course) and, although in terms of the sheer *scale* of human misery involved Lincoln was the vaster disaster, I shall never forget gazing out over a sea of stinking, soaked Lancashire hippies living in plastic bags amidst a sea of liquid mud, under a lowering sky and sheets of bucketing rain. In the far background – outlined by the Victorian factory chimneys of the neighbouring industrial wasteland – miserable lines of more hippies, most of them female, stood outside the repulsive swamps that the toilet facilities had become even before the festivities had officially opened. Onstage the while there was the crackle and zzzap as short-circuits arced and spluttered and the acts, wearing rubber ponchos, diced with death. Not a happy picture; but worse was to come, in scale at least.

For the benefit of those who do not know Lincolnshire, the country is green and very flat. (It is the nearest you ever get in England to the big skies of other lands.) As a result winds from the adjacent North Sea – or from any direction for that matter – tend to whip across East Anglia unopposed, and at consequently horrific speeds.

I think it was when I saw an entire striped marquee, ropes, tent-pegs and all, flying with enormous, stately dignity across a field – and dozens of people in vain pursuit – that I first realized that the British summer was not going to be content with the evil debacle at Bickershaw. This, by the way, was on the day *before* the festival officially opened its gates.

By the following morning, the gale had worked itself up nicely to a young hurricane. Winds were shrieking across the fields. Long-haired festival-goers began to resemble inverted Ls, as they staggered through the storm, their hair blowing out horizontally. And with the wind came the rain: even more than at Bickershaw, it seemed; no steady, remorseless downpour, but great sheets of water blowing across Lincolnshire in cloud-shaped buckets. Anyone venturing outside a marquee was instantly soaked to the skin and chilled by the wind.

The hot-air balloon scheme was the first to be called off. Later that first doomed morning, the man who was planning to high-dive from sixty feet into a pail of water also thought better of it.

The only part of the huge festival site to remain relatively immune from the worst effects of the storm was the no-go (to Joe Public, anyway) areas cordoned off for exclusive use by the promoters, acts, officials and press. Here, amid a rare grove of a few ragged trees Stanley Baker had installed his on-site HQ – a sizeable, well-appointed motor home. Where the sheikh pitches his tents, there also do the sheikh's followers and others dependent on his favour. Privilege City therefore sheltered itself, more or less, from the ravages of the wind, if not from the rain. But beyond the guarded pale, all was misery and anguish to a degree not seen in western Europe since the Somme. The bog of Bickershaw was as nothing to the lake that Lincolnshire had become. Enduring the first twenty-four hours of the Great Western

Festival without solid walls to scurry to must have been like rounding the Horn in dirty weather lashed to the jib of a square-rigger.

In the setting-up period, before the weather struck, Stanley Baker and his consortium had been putting themselves about a bit, striding purposefully hither and thither. By the end of Day 1 nothing whatever was to be seen of these truly unfortunate men – though from time to time reports would come in to the effect that a pallid, ghostlike face, mouth atwitch, had been spotted at the motor home windows (normally kept heavily shrouded); or that a ghastly hand had been seen to appear and take in the milk. It soon became clear that the weather which had so blighted their hopes of an honest profit was being widely – nay, gleefully – publicized on radio stations. As a direct result many thousands of potential punters, each representing a vital contribution to the gross – and all of whom might reasonably have been expected to make the journey had the weather been fair – were now hanging up their gumboots and stoking up the home fires. In other words, the gate, already dismally low, was more than likely to sink even lower on a *pro diem* basis. Financially the Great Western Festival was a major disaster for its promoters.

It was also pretty bad from the point of view of the acts; but that's another story.

Even when they are successful – and they usually are – promoters never take more than a tiny fraction out of the pop public cake compared with the record companies. So, bearing in mind that record companies' turnover accounts for 90 per cent of *all* music business, who exactly is into *them*, and for how much?

Well, obviously, the Revenue is into them; a fixed proportion of the price of every record, 45 rpm or LP, is set aside at source. Then there are the fees payable to the composer and performers of the product. What's left belongs to the record company, which, in classic business jargon, has fronted the entire operation, taken all the risk, covered all the expenses and overheads. If things go smoothly, a decent amount of this will be profit – and the more a record sells, the higher this proportion is likely to become; after all, once you've shipped enough units to cover your overheads, the rest is gravy, isn't it? It's called 'bringing the unit price down'.

Since the tax is the only immutable part of the breakdown, it follows that it is in the record company's interests to keep all other payments as low as possible in order to minimize the risk and increase profits. This is after all only 'good business'.

Apart from the Revenue the other two major parties into the record companies are the composers of the music and the performers. It may surprise some people to learn that the average composer's royalty may be three or more times larger than the average performer's. *Now* do you understand why artistes and acts prefer – have long preferred – to write their own songs? As singers and musicians only they might get (say) 5 per cent of the net price of each record sold; but as *composers* of the same song their slice goes up to a whopping 20 per cent plus. Good luck to them (authors could certainly use similar deals). All the same, the proportions of the split can hardly be said to have influenced music necessarily for the better. Instead of recording the best song available – and so giving an honest living to non-performing composers – acts for years have tended strongly towards the practice of recording *their own* best material. Which – to say the very least, and as we all know – may not mean much.

In addition to copping vast proportions of the net record sales by virtue of performing and composing, acts for many years now have been able to get money up-front – an advance which is set against earning from future sales. Sometimes – in the case of major, proven acts – this money will be non-returnable, a one-payment signing fee; but you have to be pretty damn proven to get that these days.

There was a time, in the late sixties and early seventies, when these advances could be staggering. The trouble was, many acts took the money and spent it on cocaine and high living before being eventually brought to book and made to sit in a studio perforce and record something – anything – that the investors could market. As by this time the acts' small store of talent had entirely been dissipated in a twelvemonth or more of the grossest self-indulgence, the resulting product was very often of highly questionable quality – only just marketable, in fact – while on certain notorious occasions the pressure-recorded *meisterwerk* was so utterly dire that not even the hardest-necked record company could take the chance. When groups break up, with one or another member going off noisily to 'do his own thing', it is often because something like this has just happened. The one who leaves most noisily is either the only one with any sense of pride, or else he is the one everybody else blames for the fiasco.

It is when you have a sulky, dissipated, near-broke combo recording their own songs under extreme and self-induced physical decline coupled with record company pressure that you get the worst music.

We all have our favourite examples of this.

However, simply making respective payments to the Revenue, to the composers, and to the performers is far too easy; into the gap a score of different types of middleman have long inserted themselves.

A major ploy for big-earning acts is to found their 'own' record label. Little actually changes. The records are still made by the same people, and the recordings are still funded, indirectly, by the parent record company. The records are distributed in exactly the same way –

all is as it was before except that now the actual discs have stickers
of a different design surrounding the hole and (most importantly) a
fiscal cut-off has now been inserted between the payer (the parent
record company) and the payee (the act), enabling the payee to pay
– in the end – less of his own share of the take to the Revenue.

Yet more cut-offs can be inserted – and some of the big earners are
so rich that one can only approve their intentions. You can now have
a management company to act as a holding company for the (subsid-
iary) record company. Meanwhile the royalties are being paid to a
publishing company set up along the same lines as the 'independent'
record company (e.g. Northern Songs, i.e. Lennon and McCartney).
These two independent companies, often but not necessarily in association with a management company, then pass on ever-decreasing
amounts of money to the actual composer and act respectively (or
together). By this time the composer's share of a multi-million selling
45 rpm disc, originally (say) £35,000, will have dwindled, via the various cut-offs, to a mere £49.70 plus luncheon vouchers. However, any
time the lucky fellow chooses to step over to the Cayman Islands, he
will be able to peruse with satisfaction bank balances and other assets
worth the missing £34,950.30; for he is a part or whole owner of all
the aforementioned cut-offs. If you insert enough cut-offs none of
them earns enough, on paper, to pay tax at all. Few acts attain this
exalted state, but many get quite close. You can see that it is sometimes
a useful device. Few if any rock and roll musicians come into the biz
knowing the first thing about finance. Mind you, some learn pretty
fast. But in learning, they tend to acquire manager-figures. Some come
into the business already tooled-up with manager-figures – as did the
Beatles. Either way, relations between acts and MFs (if I may so call
them from now on), while sometimes excellent and abiding, are often
fractious and (afterwards) litigious.

Really thrusting or super-efficient MFs quite often end up with a
permanent lifetime stake in the client; no matter what the latter does,
or where he goes, he has this monkey on his back till death do them
part. If the MF in question is red hot and a marvel of integrity (towards
the client, anyway), this can still be no bad thing *provided the parties
concerned never fall out,* that is. Untangling some of these deep-rooted
allegiances can be a protracted, expensive and acrimonious business
(e.g. Tom Parker, Allen Klein, etc.).

Even the MF of average savvy, hustle and greed can expect to be
invited, as it were, to join the board of most of the connected cut-off
or holding companies. Indeed, such outfits will probably have been his
idea, and set up by him in the first place. In addition to owning stock
in all of these (the more he hustles his clients the more stock he will
own), he will also be paid a fat director's fee for each company, and

all this will be in addition to his managerial fee, which comes off the top and is probably the original of all the many subsequent contractual bondings he and his lads have signed. So with a big-earning act, the MF of only average hustle is in Fat City.

The rest of the constituents of the music business are strictly peripheral. Not to be sniffed at are the revenues extracted from musicians (both professional and especially amateur) by the manufacturers of musical instruments and equipment. Then there are the employees – other than the MF – of the musicians, whether permanent or temporary. Most largish acts maintain a skeleton staff of two or three road managers. On tour this number will be drastically swelled by the hiring, on a daily basis, of temporary roadies – including that most demeaning of all rock and roll posts, the personal roadies (i.e. valets-cum-chauffeurs-cum-pimps-cum-drug-dealers). Other temporary staff who can expect to be taken on for tour purposes are those small, semi-independent organizations which hire out not only the vast PA and lighting systems without which the modern act feels naked on stage, but also the expert crews to install and run them.

That more or less takes care of the major chain of hand-me-down cash which began, we remember, with the general pop public all those many stages ago. However, the pop public being the limitless mother-lode that it is, other prospectors also operate their own mining schemes – and not all of these are necessarily small time.

The record companies also employ large numbers of people. PR and A&R men are the particular specialities that come to mind – though for a long time the most successful PRs and record producers (the term 'A&R' is antique) have been freelancers, often with their own organizations. Rock and roll PR is exactly the same as any other form of PR – major individuals or agencies do their best to acquire quiverfuls of acts, each of whom pays a retainer whose amount depends on a sliding scale composed, cynically, of the following increments: the fame and wealth of the client; the nominal 'standard rates' of the PR; and the client's actual ability to pay. As a consequence, workaday record company PR departments are rundown poor relations.

The people who organize and supervise recording sessions have similarly refused, largely to their profit, to remain 'in house'. In the old days of the fifties and early sixties, when A&R men ruled the studios with rods of iron, they exerted almost total domination over the proceedings. Just about every record made during that epoch is far more the product of the A&R man than of the artiste(s). But with the general secession of the richer pop groups from the parent record giants, A&R men – who for long have been calling themselves 'producers' (when actually 'directors' is a better description of what they do) – have followed the trend and moved into the prosperous shallows of freelance work. Thus, like the independent PRs, they are also employees, though on a casual, if well-paid, basis.

The music press is an excellent example of another kind of hustle. In the mid-seventies, my own magazine – then the top seller in the UK – was making over £300,000 net profit for its publishers each year. And there were then two other magazines competing directly with us, both of which had respectable sales not vastly smaller than ours. But there were, and are, a very great number of 'teeny' magazines which must also be accounted part of the music press in as much as they write about the same general area, albeit with a different slant.

Finally we come full circle – and back to the broadcasters.

The power that the music press wields over record sales is minute compared with that of the radio and TV stations – this is true anywhere in the Western world.

In the UK the position is complicated by the existence of the BBC, a public corporation which takes no advertising. Instead (Americans may not know this) it is funded by the government in the same way that the salaries of the royal family are funded. However British governments get back at least some of this money by levying TV licences: you pay the most for a colour TV, less for a black and white TV. So once again we find Joe Public – and not just Joe Pop Public – providing the working funds. Therefore BBC broadcasters are operating *their* own mining concern.

Certainly BBC pop broadcasters – disc jockeys and the like – are part of the music business. They are indeed the classic music biz type: their attitudes, their clothes, their accents, their toupees. . . . They are also quite well paid, and often supplement their BBC earnings by opening supermarkets, etc. They are in fact that rare creature, music business celebrities who are not acts. Some music writers have aimed at this satisfying role, most without success.

The power these disc jockeys wield – for nothing sells a record like an earful of it – makes them prime targets for such under-the-table hustle and corruption as still goes on. The story that inaugurated this chapter was, to date, the last open manifestation of corporate grubbiness to be revealed in the UK. Since those days BBC procedures have changed, DJs have become even more like hippie Boy Scouts than they were before, and the activities of the 'pluggers' are carefully monitored (it says here).

The public despises DJs but record companies love them.

DJs love acts but are despised by them.

DJs are also heartily despised by music writers – but give as good as they get.

Acts despise everybody except the public.

Music writers despise everybody, especially the public.

MFs despise everybody except their clients – and sometimes secretly despise *them*.

The public despises everybody *except* the acts.

And all this mass despising goes hand in glove with the the most ludicrously hypocritical emphasis on the very opposite emotion: lurve.

Against this backdrop of mass deception and self-hypnosis, what's a little corruption, you might well ask.

And you'd be right.

SEVEN

LET IT BE

Albert Goldman, author of a highly controversial (i.e. frankly condemnatory) biography of Elvis Presley, has coined what seems to be me to be the best-yet snap definition of rock and roll.

'Rock,' says Goldman, 'is nothing more than institutionalized adolescence.'

If he is right – and I believe he is – then one must ask oneself: what are the supposed fatal attractions of post-puberty that makes it so desirable to imprison oneself there for ever?

Having once been a useless and vacuous adolescent, I can say that this period of one's life is the most miserable, aimless, and awful time of all. Even today, events which took place during my adolescence can easily have the effect, if recalled unexpectedly, of making me writhe physically and groan aloud (which can be embarrassing if one is in a public place). I believe that this experience of the years 'twixt twelve and, say, twenty-five (for adolescence continues well past the age of consent) is common to all.

Far too much attention has been paid to the views of youth (*pace* chapter 3) – which can have, have had, and are still having, considerable and dangerous effects on the survival possibilities of what may be an imperfect society, but which is still arguably the best we've got or are likely to get for some time.

However, all is not lost. Rock and roll and the youth cult generally, so fearlessly iconoclastic in their time, are now, bit by bit, being subjected to a dose of their own medicine. Goldman's *Elvis*, for example, went straight for the jugular of rock and roll's George Washington. Whether or not his allegations were true – and in my opinion most of them probably were – to say there was an hysterical outpouring of excoriation would be to minimize the reaction to his book (although in justice Goldman's book about rock and roll's most sacred cow could be fairly described in the same terms). Nor was this because Goldman had attacked the memory of a dead man. After all, Hitler's memory is attacked quite often by the rock world, and in this instance at least the don't-knock-a-stiff conventions do not appear to weigh overmuch. Goldman's sin was to write a book which – if used as a basis for further meditation – had the undoubted effect of kicking away the crutch that has kept the whole twenty-five years of institutionalized adolescence in being. Knock Elvis (well, beyond a certain point, anyway) and you knock rock. Anybody not for us is agin us – and so for many Goldman became the Enemy, in a class barely below Hitler's.

But, hopeful phenomena like *Elvis* aside, I fancy the edifice may, after all, be sliding into limbo. And the reason is economic. The Western world being the way it is, most attention is paid not to those who have most to say, or live the most shining lives, but to those who have the most money to spend.

The Second World War was followed, first in America, later in Europe, by an unparalleled economic boom. There were jobs for all – well-paid jobs, at that. Any young person who wanted to earn money stood a fair chance of doing so and when you have a new, multitudinous class with lots of money to spend, you have the characters anxious to influence the purchasing. Not only that, but you have a large number of people equally eager to learn the views and if possible mould the tastes of the new free-spending subsociety – again, in order to cop a profit at the end of the day.

The recession of the seventies at first had effects almost wholly inflationary; then, as desperate Western governments grasped the nettle and instituted policies designed to transmogrify funny money into unemployment, jobs were lost as managers and manufacturers ruthlessly shed any labour that came under the heading of 'inessential'.

Since most young people, no matter how much potential they may possess, can fairly be described as inessential (in employment terms certainly), a large part of the blow fell on adolescents.

The fact that the great Monopoly game has moved on to another square and that conditions have now changed, so that a good many adolescents, through no especial fault of their own, are now quite genuinely unemployable, is ignored (both by those who actually imagine they are missing out as well as those who desire for their own mreasons to make political capital and discredit their rivals in government).

Actually, youth *is* missing out: on money.

And this newfound absence of the green and folding is now beginning to mean that, all of a sudden, the views of youth are not so important as once they were.

After all, who chases the votes of the disfranchised? Who woos a consumer who has not the wherewithal to consume?

Nobody with any brains.

Therefore youth are buying fewer records.

Record companies' profits are well down.

Acts can expect far less cash these days in the form of advances.

Monetarism – in a phrase – has given rock and roll a head-butt between the eyes and is how busily stomping on the remains.

And with the slowing-down of the carousel, the twenty-five-year-old Dream of Bozontius is beginning to turn into so much evil-smelling ectoplasm.

As I have argued throughout this book, the signs were there for those with eyes to see as far back as 1960. But some have been more in evidence than others.

A particular example of this kind of one-off smoke signal was the appearance, in 1975, on a late-night TV chat show, of the English avant-garde film director Ken Russell. Russell was on TV to promote his recent movie of the rock opera *Tommy*. This, you may remember, was in origin the brainchild of Peter Townshend, the lead guitarist of The Who, a major British rock and roll act. *Tommy* started life as a concept LP and had subsequently gone through all the phases that a successful concept can experience. Russell's transformation of the rock opera into a major movie was but the latest – and most grandiose – attempt to milk the deaf, dumb and blind pinball player's surrealistic saga of yet more mazuma.

Anyway, there he was, this thrusting, avant-garde director-figure, hair flying as he bobbed and weaved in his seat, holding forth with (even for him) unusual vehemence. About Rock.

It transpired that, in making *Tommy*, Russell had himself finally been bitten for the very first time by the Rock bug. 'I am convinced as never before,' raved the creative cineast, 'that Rock is the true basis on which the forthcoming revolution will build! Rock,' he added – and now the spittle was flying so thick and fast that one could see the chat-show host, himself no slouch at saliva-expectoration, recoiling in his padded chair – 'Rock can save the world!'

I wonder how many others viewing this exhibition thought as I did that the day the likes of Ken Russell 'discovers' rock and roll, the beast must surely be several years dead.

But we were talking about adolescence. What other characteristics are members of this age-group noted for?

How about self-righteousness and its yoke-mate, solemnity?

I was once sent by my magazine to the United States to review and interview The Yes. To cut a lot of preliminary scene-setting short, I will say at once that this is precisely the kind of freebie to which I was referring in an earlier chapter. Well, both the group and I went through our respective parts in the routine. They played, and I watched. Afterwards, I interviewed them.

Now this group above all others were known for their obsessiveness over matters of diet. They were heavily into health food (and probably still are). Promoters weaseling away on The Yes concerts were contractually obliged to provide, for the combo's consumption, vast banquets of *miso* soup, boiled cactus root, guava-bread rolls, brown-flour pizza, and untreated rats'-milk cheese, or whatever. I myself had not realized how gargantuan these spreads were until I saw band members solemnly tucking into this disgusting slop after their gig. Something about the way they guzzled the stuff gave me an idea.

My idea was to persuade the group to pose for a self-guying photograph which I felt sure could make our front cover. I may even have promised as much to the manager-figure, Brian Lane. I wanted the group to pose in front of a banquet such as I had just witnessed behaving like *absolute gannets*, with brown rice stuffed up their noses, mouths adribble with malt extract, and vegetarian tacoburgers smeared all over their cheeks. I would have this scene shot through a wide-angle lens to increase the distortion and thereby the joke.

Considering the exceptionally pious and boring stance The Yes took over just about everything – but especially health food – I was, and remain, convinced that a front cover along these lines would have done them no end of good. Lane himself – to whom I first put the idea – was mildly encouraging. He told me that when he'd interviewed Patrick Moraz, Rick Wakeman's Swiss replacement, with a view to offering him the job – one of the highest-paid keyboard jobs in rock – he'd asked him whether he was a vegetarian.

'If necessary,' replied the practical Swiss. And he got the job.

Lane went off to put my proposal to The Yes and I waited. Eventually I was summoned. Three of the band's innermost, guiding cabal sat on a bed watching me with sad spaniel eyes – and I knew I'd got the thumbs-down.

'We've considered tha proposal,' said vocalist Jon Anderson (a Lancashire lad), 'and we've got ta tell thee that we don't feel able to go along wi' it.' Formal, you see – sincere. No cries of 'Bollocks!' which – had I been in their shoes – would have better served their case. No, they had to tell me there and then how sincere they were about the grub they ate, and how deeply they hoped to influence their fans into adopting similar dietary patterns.

There was also an air of suspicion present – almost as if they thought I was trying to talk them into making idiots of themselves. which of course I was – but, for once, in the act's best interests as I conceived them to be.

On the other hand, the absurd solemnities of institutionalized adolescence can often lead the perpetrators thereof into oubliettes of disaster.

Take John Lennon.

Probably Lennon's most famous single tune – certainly since the formal demise of the Beatles – was, and is, 'Imagine'.

> Imagine no possessions,
> I wonder if you can . . .

it begins, and on first hearing these words, I said to myself, wonder if *you* can, John, old mate. Especially since the promotional film made at the time showed Lennon and wife Yoko Ono (a) wandering through the grounds of a fabulously expensive Surrey mansion, (b) posing in ridiculous (but fabulously expensive) clothes outside the actual fab edifice, and (c) playing a ten-thousand-dollar (i.e. fabulously expensive) white grand piano. Not for the first time in human history, therefore, those who urged the no-possessions option upon their admirers and followers were themselves visibly richer than Croesus. Nor – being at bottom eminently practical, no matter how gonzo-hypocritical they were – did the Lennons ever part with significant amounts of their loot. Lennon's slightly later removal to New York may well have been because of that city's more vibrant cultural atmosphere, etc., but it is also worth noting that US residents – especially those in the Lennons' earning bracket – pay considerably less income tax than their opposite numbers in the UK. And in due course, when poor old John Lennon fell to the sidewalk riddled with bullets, his last will and testament showed that despite the money he'd spent on whimsy, fancy and various hard drugs during the middle seventies, he was still rich enough to leave several hundred million dollars. It also turned out that He Who Wondered If We Could Imagine No Possessions owned a prize herd of cattle somewhere in upstate New York – substitute racehorses for heifers and we could be talking about the Aga Khan.

Mind you, John Lennon had a heart of gold. Everybody said so, especially those on their way to the prestigious Dakota Building (where Lennon lived) in order to persuade the Committed Beatle to contribute, either cash or presence, to some cause or other. And Lennon – who by now fancied himself like mad in the role of Number One Touch in the Western Hemisphere – barely baulked at supporting each and every cause that was drawn to his attention.

As is well known, he sent back his MBE because of Britain's covert support of the federal side during the Nigerian civil wars. Less well known is the fact that my own father was one of the empurpled former majors who sent *his* back in protest at Lennon copping an MBE in the first place; both gestures, in my opinion, were adolescent.

He – Lennon, that is, not my father – supported feminism and anti-racism, adroitly coupling these two modern causes together in a single song, title 'Woman Is the Nigger of the World' (yes, and niggers' women do worse than most).

Like many New Yorkers, he supported Irish Republicanism whole-heartedly. The less said about *that* the better, I guess, since the objects of his admiration continue to assassinate people on a daily basis – in fact, the way in which J.L. himself met his demise was identical, in style if not motive, to the way in which many innocent men, women and even children have met their deaths at the hands of Lennon's protégés. Instant karma!

For a while it seemed as if nothing was beyond the pale for John. He even lent well-publicized moral support to one Michael Abdul Malik, otherwise known as Michael X (after Malcolm X), a leader of the British faction of Black Power during the early seventies. X's fortunes were then at a low ebb – most black folks in Britain having seen through him – but were conveniently resuscitated by Lennon's seal of approval (he actually went to stay with X). Shortly afterwards X murdered a white girl in Trinidad, and was duly convicted and executed.

But a major reason – second only to the economics of the thing – why the institutionalized adolescence of rock and roll failed to receive, from society at large, the kick in the crotch that would have put it properly in its place . . . is sex.

Sex! If ever rock and roll was about anything at all, it was, and is, about sex. We have already mentioned the dim-witted stud-figure swaying his snake hips and fingering the length of hosepipe stuffed down his trousers. To which we might add the legions of dim-witted post-pubescent females swaying and baying and pretending to secrete intimate juices into their underwear.

The average Beatles concert in the mid-sixties, for example, was positively torrid with sexual atmosphere. As were Elvis gigs, and a great many performances by other artistes. The Doors' Jim Morrison, for example, flashed his nudger onstage in one of the Deep South states and was promptly incarcerated by the local gendarmerie. At this, there was an outcry. But really, what did people expect? If you or I produce our peters, say, in Waterloo Station during the commuter rush, we can safely expect to have our collars felt; and pronto. But Morrison was always a grotesque character. Revelling in his self-bestowed *nom de pénis* of 'The Lizard King', he was well known – oddly in view of the 'sexually honest' hippie era in which he and his band made the big time – for overt, contemptuous sexual display onstage. These displays were grosser by far than anything ever produced in public by the originator of the whole thing, Elvis Presley. Just as sexually explicit – but somehow with more style – was the early Guitar Hero Jimi Hendrix, the highlight of whose act was a simulated copulation with his Fender Stratocaster guitar. He did it quite well, mind you, with a nice, easy action that many a middle-aged has-been might admire.

And here lies the key to society's failure to ignore the rock and roll phenomenon, which – with hindsight – is probably the only technique that would have successfully exorcised it, or at least kept it within bounds. Sexual envy.

Doctors tell us that males are at their sexual peak – in terms of stamina, anyway – at the age of seventeen. It is also held – wrongly in my view – that females are at their prettiest at the same age. It is my contention that, whatever middle-aged (or at least post-adolescent) fans of rock and roll *think* are their reasons for taking such an interest in rock and roll and its attendant culture, the *real* reason is that they envy the rampant adolescents their supposed sexual potency and powers of attraction. Conversely, those who have so bitterly attacked rock and roll from the days of its inception – people like Billy Graham and Moral Majority crusaders – are also obsessed, in the reverse sense, by the same fundamental twitches. Thus a major reason for rock's twenty-five years of popularity has been the lack of sexual self-confidence possessed by the older generation.

You *can* feel pain and bliss as an adolescent *inamorato*. You can also catch influenza. Nobody would expect a flu-stricken 'teen' thenceforth to be an expert on viral infections – so why accept his protestations that he knows all there is to know about the most mysterious, exalted and abiding of all human experiences? And yet this is precisely what society *was* told to accept, over and over again, especially in the hippie era. 'All you need is love,' they sang, shaking their heads sadly at those older bozos who persisted in regarding this as a simplistic answer to the problems of humankind – and meanwhile fumbling like mad at the buttons of each others' artistically patched denims.

Humbug? You bet. The only mystery is why it all went on so long.

No endeavour should be allowed to regard itself as an Art Form so quickly.

And then – leaving aside the hippie rubbish – there are the numerous examples – heartening in their way – of how very rich young men can rapidly ditch the supposed love ingredient and get right down to the business of making sexual beasts of themselves – aided and abetted, I ought to say, by that scaly class of insecure nymphomaniacs traditionally known as 'groupies'.

There is the famous (and actually rather talented) Guitar Hero who enjoyed tying groupies up in barbed wire. (No, no names, no pack drill.)

Then we have a whole series of idiotic and unpleasant tableaux: John Lennon being ejected from Los Angeles' Troubador Club for wearing a sanitary napkin on his head. ('Do you know who I am?' he expostulated. 'Yes, you're some asshole with a Kotex on his head,' replied the waitress who occasioned the ejecting.) In the same throbbing nitespot, you might – on an earlier occasion – have seen The Who's drummer Keith Moon grinning like a baboon while some desperate little girl performed public fellatio on him – cheered on without a trace of embarrassment by a crowd of people who would undoubtedly have described themselves as 'beautiful'.

Yet another anecdote. I once went to New York in my 'professional' capacity, with a well-known British combo (no, not The Yes – this was slightly before their time). Their prestigious concert at Madison Square Garden being completed, we all returned to the prestigious downtown hotel. There the evening's licentiousness really got under way. Being a mere journalist – and therefore way below even the ugliest roadie in the pecking order – none of the female hangers-on made a bid for *my* services and, half disappointed, half relieved, I prepared to turn in. Then I got a call. Come to such-and-such a suite. I did so. What I found were the group, their MF, and a couple of their senior roadies, all bollock-naked, engaged in copulatory pursuits. Bare breasts, bare bottoms, dangling phalli . . . not a fleshly ingredient was missing. The drummer was operating across the television set; others had settled for couches, or carpeted corners. On the central table was a sheet of paper with a vast white cone of cocaine – about two thousand dollars' worth, I guessed. Alongside the 'charlie' was a large paper sack full of cannabis. Underneath the table was a crate of Remy Martin cognac.

And not a smile on anybody's face.

Whatever I say I'm going to end up sounding like a prude or a hypocrite (like the tabloid investigative reporters who 'make their excuses and leave'), so I had better make it clear that, taken in isolation, there was nothing in the room that I particularly objected to. Cocaine is not my favourite drug – six hours of self-opinionated bad temper seems to be too high a price to pay for five minutes of feeling mentally invincible – but I have always been rather fond of weed, whatever its name is this year. And Remy Martin is a superb cognac. Nor do I object to sexual intercourse, especially when it involves myself. What *was* abhorrent was the air of desperation; the all-embracing feeling that we've-got-all-this-money-so-let's-pig-it-as-much-as-we-can . . . it was barely surprising that the essential innocence of enjoyment was missing. The characters concerned had done it all before, many times. While making a pig out of yourself and others is usually fun the first time one does it, as a regular activity it tends to pall. On this occasion it had already reached the palling stage long before, yet none of the participants had allowed him- or herself to get the message. Nothing exceeds like excess, they say.

So, having taken a snort of the 'charlie', and grabbed a major handful of the weed and appropriated a half-full bottle of the Remy, I made my excuses and left.

Speaking of the palling process, I fancy that when combos run wild in hotel rooms, enraging fellow-guests (who have seldom done them the slightest harm) and causing hotel staff acute worry and stress, it is because they've reached the stage where they can have all they want and still don't want it. What's left but to bung a TV set through a seventeenth floor window; and if it falls on some citizen's head – why, the MF will pay him off fast enough.

Mind you, rock and roll stardom sometimes has the opposite effect: it stimulates the getting of religion. Or fails to protect against it, if you prefer.

Here we have a complex phenomenon, deriving from a variety of causes. For example, in the case of Little Richard, the major factor in his highly publicized Born-Againism was undoubtedly his Deep South, Baptist upbringing. In his heart Small Dick has clearly always believed that rock and roll *is* 'the Devil's music' – otherwise why, when travelling in an aircraft that he thought was about to crash, did he promise to give up rock and roll if the good Lord would only get him down in one piece? I too am a lousy aeronaut, ready to promise anything to anybody if I can be got down in one piece; *in extremis* most of us toady like mad. But what is significant is that Little Richard, in his understandable terror, zeroed in on the one thing he must have been convinced he had long been doing wrong.

For me, Christianity, as a religion, has always been . . . well, un-convincing. The only thing that can be said for it, in my view, is that, no matter how much I or others may find it simplistic and feeble-minded, the undeniable fact is that historically it underpins our culture. Whatever the state of Western Civilization these days, to discuss it at all and not mention Christianity is pointless. The two go together like hamburger and bun.

So why, whenever Christianity manifests itself in some rock celebri-ty's life, does it appear so thoroughly idiotic? Little Richard is off the hook on account of his early conditioning; but what can one say of the Anglo-Indian pop star Cliff Richard, the earliest (and in his day, the most convincing) of UK Elvis clones, who saw the light very early on and ever since, on his own claims, has remained celibate? Who exactly does he think he's pleasing by laying off the soft and lissome in this early-medieval, self-denying way?

Mind you, Cliff Richard does stay eerily young; in fact, although he's now over forty, he doesn't appear to have aged at all in the last twenty years. Maybe he knows something we don't . . . but I doubt it.

However, nobody would deny Cliff Richard's absolute right to follow whatever inner call makes him most comfortable; certainly his faith is harmless (except when he lends his weight to the moral-censor brigade, as he does all too often). The same cannot be said of other rock and roll religiosos.

Take Islam.

Yes, the faith of the Prophet, born in desert sands amid the fierce Bedouin, nourished in a cauldron of blood, and gleefully proselytized throughout the Middle and Near East in the five centuries between the Prophet Mohammed falling on his head and the Christian champion El Cid charging along the beach, stone-dead and dressed as Charlton Heston. In many ways this religion is a clone of Christianity; certainly both have plenty of blood on their hands. Nowadays convention forbids us to mock another's religion. To hell with convention: in its modern reconstructed form, Islam appears to mean xenophobia, distortion and tyranny.

Islam had a bout of fashionability in the West in the late sixties and early seventies. The most famous converts were of course the Black Muslims; while perhaps its most celebrated single convert is Muhammad Ali, alias Cassius Clay, the heavyweight pugilist. But rock and roll people were not immune, either – and whereas there's a certain race-origin justification for American blacks to adopt the faith of the Prophet (which has always been especially widespread in West Africa, whence most of their ancestors came), the very idea of conversion becomes bizarre in the extreme when the Anglo-Greek pop singer Cat Stevens (he of 'I'm Gonna Get Me A Gun'), and the purely Anglo folk-music duo Richard and Linda Thompson take it up.

In case I should be misunderstood, my point is not merely that rock and roll – with its supposedly virtuous and far-sighted lifestyle – fails to *protect* its adherents from all-round religious goofiness, but that in many instances the attendant excesses (especially true at the top), actively *encourage* it. Probably about the same percentage of free-thinking, love-making, clear-eyed and committed alternative lifestylists (rock and roll is stiff with them) end up in the loony-religious outer fringe as those originating from 'straight' (contemptuous and moreover inaccurate word) society at large; but where the odd doings of a community of, say, extreme Baptists might attract no more than average attention, the pronouncements and attitudes of a good many rock and roll performers are, as has been described, of consuming interest to many and as a result are widely and repeatedly publicized.

But there are worse things than oafish stupidity. One of the most infamous mass-murderers of the last two decades, Charles Manson, was apparently motivated by deep religious convictions which seemingly centred around himself. And this time there is no escaping the connection between religious barminess and rock and roll, since Manson was *directly inspired* in his awfulness by Beatles lyrics – particularly, we are told, George Harrison's 'Piggies' and Lennon and McCartney's 'Helter Skelter'. No blame to the Beatles concerned for Manson's actions, of course (Hitler was a Bernard Shaw-inspired vegetarian, come to think of it), but yet again we see the rock and roll lifestyle, with all its moralizing, failing to provide even elementary protection against life's lousier hands of cards. Most of all, for its adherents who fail to think it through. Perhaps more thinking of itself as 'it' and almighty.

In which connection it is worth restating that it was for love of the Lord that Mark David Chapman bumped off John Ono Lennon.

Luckily most of the religiously inspired barminess is on a lighter note. Take the Eastern religions – in their heyday, pure unsurpassed buffoonery of the very highest standards. It seems reasonable to claim that the mass interest in oriental mysticism came about through the interest in that peculiar and complicated instrument, the sitar. This twangy object made its Western disc debut in the mid-sixties; and before long its most famous near-exponent, Beatle George, was shlepping around looking like Jesus Christ on a mushroom binge and burbling about Shiva (or was it Kali? Come to think of it, it might have been Krishna). Knackered copies of unreadable books by Herman Hesse appeared and were ostentatiously pored over in public. From the occidental's point of view, the entire three-thousand-year history of Eastern religion boiled down to:

> Playing the sitar
> Carrying around a copy of *Journey to the East*
>   and
> Taking lots and lots of LSD

and in case anybody thinks this is all building up to a sneer – a reasonable assumption – let me say that in my view this is about all the three-thousand-year history of Eastern religion is worth.

Unless you could crack it as a paid-up guru. Then it was suddenly worth a whole lot more.

Most renowned of all the oriental sages to get violently rich in the heyday of TM (as we must now refer to Transcendental Meditation) was the aged, giggling Maharishi Mahesh Yogi ('Buttons' to his friends). At one time Buttons had, as customers:

> All four Beatles
> An equivalent number of Beatle women
> A Beach Boy or two
>   and
> Mia Farrow, the well-known actress.

The first to hightail it outta there was Beatle *batteriste* Ringo Starr, who fled Buttons' palatial Indian villa snorting that it was all too much like Butlin's. McCartney – we later learned – was never that convinced in the first place; while Lennon – always a sap for a new lick – went into it wholeheartedly and came out with much sound and fury. But the brace of Beach Boys hung in there with true surfin' grit – and I believe are still 'into' TM.

But first in, last out, they say, and true to form the grittiest adherent of all in the matter of Eastern mystical hotchpotch was Beatle George Harrison. It was he, after all, who had roped in his colleagues in the first place – and he who hung on to it the longest. For years after the formal dissolution of the renowned combo he was making dreary solo long-players, almost all of them dedicated to the Lord Krishna (why not the Lord Grade?). Harrison's skills on guitar, actually quite considerable, were dulled in favour of insipid lyrics extolling this or that virtue of the many-armed Aryan deity. The Lord Krishna's influence did not prove sufficient to prevent the very dreariest of these tunes, 'My Sweet Lord', from being adjudged, in a US court of law, a flagrant, plagiaristic rip-off of an earlier pop tune called 'He's So Fine': and the unhappy disciple was obliged, after fighting the case tooth, nail and joss stick, to fork out.

Perhaps the most grotesque form of the Eastern nonsense was, and is, the cult known as Krishna Consciousness, or (to non-members) as 'the saffron loonies'.

Not only is this tribe a pain in the collective buttock, they're also ugly as sin. Why wear dirty yellow gowns? Why shave the pate? Why shake bloody tambourines all day long? An especially gormless note is struck by the fact that the song they 'sing' in the street – 'Hare Krishna' – is no ancient chant from the *Rig Veda*, older than time itself, etc., but a pop hit from the sixties musical *Hair*. A parallel would be for the Pope to conduct High Mass at St Peter's while the Vatican Boys' Choir sang 'Jesus Christ Superstar'.

However, not everything to do with Eastern mysticism is gormless. The saffron loonies may make twerps of themselves in the street on a daily basis, but at the very top of this tree we have the aforementioned gurus. I name no names in this context, but despite the self-abnegation that is the central core of most Yoga variants, the TM people have managed to amass, over the years, a not inconsiderable amount of cash – enough to buy outright one of England's statelier homes. (It was when I heard about this purchase that I first seriously considered taking up TM – as a guru, of course.)

So much for religion.

In fact, so much for all of it.

Just as the first draft of this little book was nearing completion, a chap I know – a local yokel – breezed into my little shack bearing hot news.

'Oy!' he said. 'Ain't you writin' a book slaggin' orf rock an' roll an' that?'

Considering he had never read so much as a single word of the manuscript, this wasn't bad as snap definitions go. I acknowledged the general accuracy of his line of inquiry.

'Well then,' he said. 'I'd get yerself down the bookshop. Some geezer's gone an' done it already – what you're doin', I mean.'

Rifle bullets move like snails with hangovers compared with the speed I then showed in getting myself down the local bookshop. Sure enough, just as my bucolic pal had intimated, there was a new large-format rock book sitting smugly on the shelves. I can't remember the title (that's a lie, actually, but I'm sure you understand). Feverishly I grabbed the thing and riffled its pages. My little heart went pit-a-pat and my guts sank into my wellies. At first sight, sure enough, this accursed volume seemed to be attempting what I myself had already blueprinted as a certain path to riches. The general tone seemed condemnatory, and the pictures verged on the scandalous.

Curses! Beaten to the punch! In my imagination the bailiff's wagon throbbed toxically as it rumbled down the well-worn track towards my little home.

Then I read the very first sentence in the book's Foreword. It said: 'I should make it clear from the outset that I love rock 'n' roll.'

I read this again to make quite sure.

'I should make it clear from the outset that I love rock 'n' roll.'

Ever heard a sigh of relief mingled with a snort of contempt? It's some noise, I can tell you.

Apart from the telltale ' 'n' ' instead of the approved conjunction – a sure sign of a sentimental dork, and *the* reason why I myself have sternly eschewed such usage throughout this book – this sentence alone makes the writer's position quite clear. The man had shot himself through the foot. How on earth can anyone 'love' rock and roll and still hope to write a book slagging it off? Come to think of it, how on earth can anyone love rock and roll at all? Well, yes, I know – plenty do. I have myself, God help me. But by taking up this position right at the start, the writer of the aforementioned book (otherwise quite a natty piece of work, especially picture-wise) had made it quite impossible for himself to carry out his chosen brief with any hope of credibility.

So, once again – and in the unlikely event that the message has thus far failed to permeate the skull of you, the reader – let me say: I do *not* love rock and roll.

I hate rock and roll.

Rock and roll *did* exist – for about three years. It lasted about as long as the hula hoop, the yo-yo and the skateboard put together. It has just about as much long-term meaning.

It died, but rose from the grave, hideous and draped in mouldering shroud linen. Clacking its teeth together, it stalked off into the long night of Western decline, to wreak its *nosferatu*-style revenge.

And a lot of people have wasted a lot of time and money as a result.

Those who have participated in it have seen themselves as crusaders in the cause of happiness, sexual freedom, freedom generally and being nice.

As for what they actually did – no matter how they have seen themselves – this book has attempted to put the record straight.

They have made themselves ridiculous. Others in different walks of life do this, of course, but never perhaps with so little realization of their true position.

They have killed themselves with reasonable frequency. Again, others manage to pull this off, but usually with some foreknowledge of what may lie in store.

They have engaged in the most fantastic hypocrisies. Once more, hypocrisy is no phenomenon exclusive to rock and roll, but surely no movement in human history has been so fiercely *against* hypocrisy – and at the same time managed to serve as so exemplary a model of the thing to which it is nominally opposed?

Rock and rollers, wearing their 'committed' hat, have dabbled disastrously – and with a self-righteousness absolutely unparalleled in recent annals – in contemporary politics. The only result of their clear-eyed meddling has been a steady decline in the geopolitical position of the culture zone that nourished them – and the indirect advancement of the forces of unrighteousness. Despite the enormous weight of evidence to this effect, they absolutely refuse to square up to this fact. Meanwhile various other creeps, of a type well known and documented throughout history, are continuing to manipulate the ever-manipulable rock and roll faithful for other ends; not least among these being the creation of a world order in which rock and roll, to name but one movement, will have no place whatever.

Despite their 'commitment' to a sweeping-away of bourgeois virtues, rock and rollers have repeatedly demonstrated, both individually and in the mass, a penchant for pretension and pseudery that would make the most dyed-in-the-wool art-world faker gasp in envy and astonishment; all this in the name of a supposedly superior 'alternative' culture.

Other virtues that have flourished within the perimeter of rock culture have been hackery, cynicism, business fiddling, gross indulgence in 'substances', overeating, bullying of employees, patronizing of the simple-minded rock public, lack of self-respect and an abiding obsession with self. Not for nothing was the New Generation also called the Me Generation.

The rock masses have swayed this way and that, fickle almost beyond belief. Name the cause and rock has supported it. Name the badge or the T-shirt and it has been worn *en masse*.

The only remaining problem is: what to do about it?

There you have me. I don't know *what* to do about it. I suspect that nothing whatever *can* be 'done' about it – if by 'done' one means passing laws and statutes or duffing-up. The great rock and roll swindle is a symptom, not a cause, of a mass failure of nerve on the part of Western society – a condition which may – just may – be beginning to pass.

Obviously, when one sees a whole generation making a toadstool of itself, one is tempted to 'do' something; and here lies the reason for the failure of anti-rock and roll movements of the past. They all wanted to suppress the stuff, not appreciating the cardinal fact that suppression is the last thing one ought to do. (Has the Russians' suppression of Christianity caused it to blow away? No. Pity.) In my view the thing has to run its course. So far its course has lasted twenty-five years or so – longer, I guess, than many expected, myself included. But here we are, twenty-five years have passed, and rock and roll is still with us.

Or is it?

Perhaps it is beginning to fade. Three generations have now had their fling – each with their own distinguishing characteristic. Mindless anarchy (albeit with a joyful slant) was followed by fierce commitment. This has now given way to the third generation, mindless anarchy (with a pessimistic slant). The wheel has turned full circle, or nearly.

These days one no longer even hears the term 'rock and roll' with quite such frequency. Already people are beginning to talk about 'pop music' once again – a symptom of the benign change I fancy may be in the wind.

Imagine if pop music catches on! Think what that will mean! Can you imagine anyone saying 'I'm, er, doing a concert for Pop Against Racism'?

Don't knock the pop! Now *there*'s a slogan I could go for!

I've always liked pop music, provided it was pop music I thought I was liking. No one can get uptight about pop music, except for the usual mundane exceptions (transistors on beaches, etc.). Popular music is quite simply music that is currently popular – e.g. 'Greensleeves', 'Daisy, Daisy' – and by no stretch of the imagination am I against music or even popularity. Besides, the resuscitation of this valuable term surely implies that, after years out in the cold, Tin Pan Alley is once more reclaiming its inheritance. We are back in the safe world of the agent's audition, the balding Shylock with the bent contract, the tinsel, the gloss and the amiable fakery of show business. Boy (and girl) geniuses were ripped off then, and will be in this dewy future. But at least the roles will be more clearly understood by all concerned.

We can get on with our lives without being sidetracked by crippled philosophies and dangerous mass movements.

OK, so a few ambitious simpletons will continue to be exploited. So what? It is the fate of ambitious simpletons to be exploited and, if they survive the process, to become, in time, exploiters themselves.

It's called evolution.

One day I might make it.

Goodbye.